JERUSALEM PRAYER TEAM

Dear Annie,

To my beloved friend and partner. Together we are doing a great work for God.

Mike Evans

DR. MICHAEL D. EVANS

WHY WAS
I BORN?

#1 *NEW YORK TIMES* BESTSELLING AUTHOR

MIKE EVANS

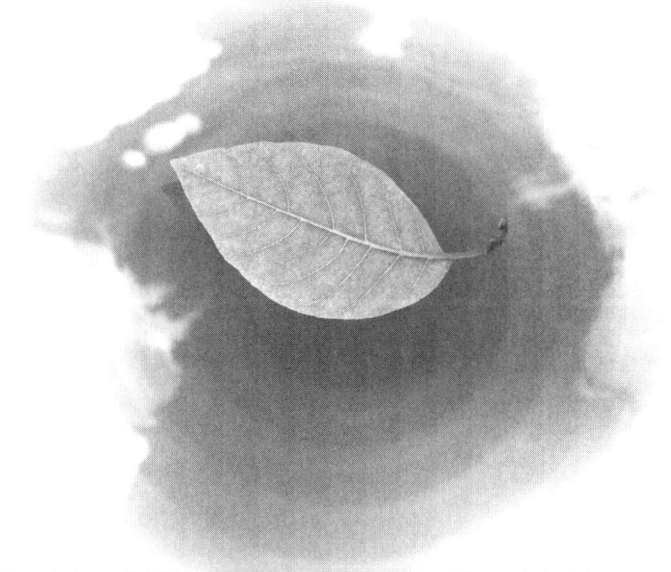

WHY WAS I BORN?

DISCOVER GOD'S PURPOSE FOR LIVING

TimeWorthy
BOOKS

P.O. Box 30000, Phoenix, AZ 85046

Why Was I Born?

Copyright © 2017
All rights reserved Printed in the United States of America

Published by TimeWorthy Books
P. O. Box 30000
Phoenix, AZ 85046

Scripture quotations marked (Nkjv) are taken from *The New King James Version* of the Bible. Copyright © 1979, 1980, 1982, 1983, 1984 by Thomas Nelson, Inc. Publishers. Used by permission.

Scripture quotations marked (AMP) are from the Amplified Bible. Old Testament copyright © and New Testament copyright © are by the Lockman Foundation. Used by permission.

Scripture quotations marked (Nlt) are taken from the *Holy Bible*, New Living Translation, copyright © 1996, 2004, 2007. Used by permission of Tyndale House Publishers Inc., Carol Stream, Illinois, 60188. All rights reserved.

Scripture quotations marked (Kjv) are taken from the *King James Version* of the Holy Bible.

Scripture quotations marked (NASB) are taken from the New American Standard Bible. Copyright © 1960, 1962, 1963, 1968, 1971, 1972, 1973, 1975, 1977, 1995 by The Lockman Foundation. Used by permission. www.Lockman.org

Scripture quotations marked (Esv) are taken from the *Holy Bible, English Standard Version*, copyright © 2001, 2007, 2011 by Crossway Bibles, a division of Good News Publishers. Used by permission. All rights reserved.

Scripture taken from *The Message* (MSG). Copyright © 1993, 1994, 1995, 1996, 2000, 2001, 2002. Used by permission of NavPress Publishing Group.

The Hebrew Names Version (HNV) is based off the World English Bible, an update of the American Standard Version of 1901. This version of the Bible is in the public domain.

Design: Peter Gloege | LOOK Design Studio

Hardcover: 978-1-62961-137-2
Paperback: 978-1-62961-138-9
   Canada: 978-1-62961-139-6

This book is dedicated to my beloved friend
and prayer partner of thirty-five years,
James G. Watt.
Jim was appointed Secretary of the Interior by
President Ronald Reagan and served from 1981 to 1983.
I deeply value his friendship.

1 ::	DON'T BE AFRAID OF THE RATS	9
2 ::	I DON'T WANT TO FEED THE PIGEONS!	21
3 ::	YOU'RE A GOOD BOY	33
4 ::	BILLY GRAHAM, THE POPE, AND ADOLF HITLER ARE ALL CHRISTIANS	53
5 ::	YES, MY SON	73
6 ::	THIS IS THE MORON	87
7 ::	I WILL BEAT YOU TO DEATH! GOD HATES LIARS	101
8 ::	YOU WILL NEVER AMOUNT TO ANYTHING	117
9 ::	WHEN I GROW UP . . . I WANT TO BE TWENTY	133
10 ::	STOP IT!!	145
11 ::	A BRIGHT LIGHT IN A DARK ROOM	157
12 ::	NAIL SCARS AND SMILING EYES	167
13 ::	HE CALLED ME 'SON'	177
14 ::	I LOVE YOU!	187
15 ::	I HAVE A GREAT PLAN FOR YOUR LIFE	199
16 ::	THE CONCLUSION OF MY FATHER'S STORY...	219
17 ::	FORGIVENESS	241
	ENDNOTES	251
	AUTHOR BIO	255

ECCLESIASTES 3:1-8 (KJV)

To every thing there is a season,
and a time to every purpose under the heaven:

A time to be born, and a time to die; a time to plant,
and a time to pluck up that which is planted;

A time to kill, and a time to heal;
a time to break down, and a time to build up;

A time to weep, and a time to laugh;
a time to mourn, and a time to dance;

A time to cast away stones, and
a time to gather stones together; a time to embrace,
and a time to refrain from embracing;

A time to get, and a time to lose;
a time to keep, and a time to cast away;

A time to rend, and a time to sew;
a time to keep silence, and a time to speak;

A time to love, and a time to hate;
a time of war, and a time of peace.

(EMPHASIS MINE)

1

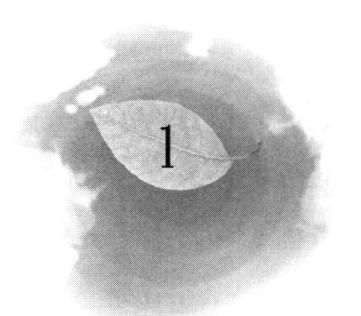

DON'T BE AFRAID OF THE RATS

(THE THINGS THAT HINDER YOU)

To say that my father was a hard and angry man would be—like Newton's law of gravitation—an unassailable truth. When angered, his blue eyes would turn to ice and his voice to steel, especially when he had his fill of Jack Daniel's and goofballs[1]. He ruled our household with a rod of iron—or a coat hanger, a belt, an electric cord—whatever was handy to inflict pain and punishment.

Dad was born in 1920 on a hardscrabble farm in Geneva, Alabama. His name was Robert, but everybody called him "Bob" to his face and "Wally," the name of a cartoon character, behind his back. He learned early at the hand of my Grandfather Will that disobedience, real or perceived, brought swift retribution. Will Evans, who had learned from his father, was also an abusive man who ultimately passed that curse along to his son, my father.

As a seven-year-old boy, Dad was forced to plow rows of peanuts and cotton behind a mule all day long in the hot Alabama sun. He could barely reach the crosspiece on the turning plow to hang on as the animal dragged him down one row and up the next. His father, tobacco juice dribbling down his chin, sat under a tree at the edge of the field. In one hand he grasped a long rope; in the other was a jug of white lightnin'. If Dad flagged or the mule stopped, Will slowly rose, fed out the rope, and walked just far enough to be able to reach Dad with the rope. Twirling it like a whip, he would unleash the coil to snap Dad on his sweat-soaked back. Reeling the rope in, he would again set it in motion to pop the mule on the flank and urge it forward. Boy and mule would set out again across the field in an effort to please the tyrant watching over them. This was my dad's early example of a father's care and concern. It was events such as these that shaped my father's life and his relationship with his children.

When I was six years old, my father operated a John Deere bulldozer at the local dump. From early morning to closing time, he dug holes, pushed trash into them, and then it was burned. After the flames were extinguished,

Dad would bury the remains. When he saw that the grocery stores had thrown daily foodstuff into the dumpsters, he would sort through it and bring any salvageable goods home. Our family was very poor, lived in the Projects, and much of our food was scavenged from the dump.

One morning, I accompanied him to work. I quickly spied boxes of "white" chocolate that had been thrown away. What I didn't know was that it was dark chocolate that had turned white because of age. I climbed over piles of trash to retrieve it, and as I reached out, rats emerged from beneath the garbage. I shuddered and screamed in terror. Suddenly, an elderly black man sitting in a nearby chair smiled and handed me a stick. I looked up at him and saw that he had only two front teeth. He cautioned me, "Don't be afraid of the rats. They are just as afraid of you as you are of them." I took the stick from him, grasped it as I would a baseball bat, and swung as hard as my six-year-old arms could swing it. I connected with a pile of the garbage, and as I did, the rats ran!

The fear of the unknown can be a devastating hindrance. I feared the unknown when reaching for the boxes of chocolate; however, once I was armed with an offensive weapon, that fear disappeared. The biblical David had learned those lessons in the sheepcote armed with a sling and a staff. It would be critical when he faced one of the most decisive battles of his life: against the giant of Gath! David learned the first thing to do when trouble emerges: Trust God!

After David was anointed by Samuel, there came a morning when his father, Jesse, ordered his youngest son to take supplies to his brothers who were battling the Philistines in the Valley of Elah. Upon his arrival, David beheld the imposing figure of Goliath and heard the challenge being hurled across the valley to his quaking audience on the other side. David was incensed that no one in King Saul's army had the courage to face the giant. They all stood on the sidelines, intimidated by the ferocity of the huge warrior. David was not foolhardy; he knew beyond a doubt that only through the power of God could anyone defeat this adversary. He asked those around him what would be the reward for the one who slayed the enemy. David's brothers were angered by his question and began to ridicule him. He then marched before Saul and offered to fight the giant.

When Saul questioned both his youth and ability, David replied:

> "I have been taking care of my father's sheep and goats . . . . When a lion or a bear comes to steal a lamb from the flock, I go

after it with a club and rescue the lamb from its mouth. If the animal turns on me, I catch it by the jaw and club it to death. I have done this to both lions and bears, and I'll do it to this pagan Philistine, too, for he has defied the armies of the living God! The Lord who rescued me from the claws of the lion and the bear will rescue me from this Philistine!" (Samuel 17:34–37 NLT)

David was a man of great humility; he knew that he was unable to do anything except through the power of God. He declined to accept any commendation for his feats; he gave God the credit. He boldly assured Saul that God would stand with the man who dared go forth in His name; that God would give that man victory. In humility, David offered himself as an instrument in his Father's hands.

King Saul offered David his personal armor for the battle with Goliath. After having tried it on, the young man realized that the covering fashioned by mortal hands was insufficient for the task. Like the apostle Paul, David understood that he was only safe when covered with the full armor of God. He would be vulnerable in Saul's armor; he would be invincible wrapped in the presence of Jehovah-Sabaoth—the Lord our Protector.

The lack of vision can be equally hindering. My friend the late pastor and evangelist Myles Munroe defined vision as "the idea that never leaves you, the dream that won't go away and the passion that won't subside."[2] No matter how often discouragement knocks on your door, no matter how demanding the circumstances, your God-given vision will propel you forward toward your goal. With faith and tenacity, you will reap the reward.

The apostle Paul wrote in Philippians 3:13–14 (NKJV):

> Brethren, I do not count myself to have apprehended; but one thing I do, forgetting those things which are behind and reaching forward to those things which are ahead, I press toward the goal for the prize of the upward call of God in Christ Jesus.

My wife, Carolyn, taught me a faith lesson when our last child was born. I had secretly wanted a son to love, probably because I never had a father who loved me. I thought I would only have my three beautiful daughters, which was fine with me. They are my sweethearts! But God gave Carolyn and me another child. Carolyn obstinately refused to listen to the opinions of others—those who told her she would have another girl. She believed God had told her a boy was on the way. Let me repeat that: She believed God! She was totally convinced, against all odds, that our baby would be a boy and declared that he would be named Michael David Evans II. I reminded Carolyn that I didn't have a middle name. Of course, it didn't faze her at all; the new mother won that battle. Soon thereafter, I appeared before a judge to have my name changed to Michael David Evans. Both my son and I are now named "David" as are hundreds and thousands of boys and their fathers worldwide. I later told my son, "I was named after you. When I grow up, I want to be just like you."

This book is special to me; I wanted it to be our book—mine and yours. I want us to delve deeply into the Scriptures and ask God to reveal the principles that will light a fire in our bones. Over the years, I have traveled millions of miles—from the Kremlin Palace in Moscow to the Royal Palace in Madrid. I have met popes, princes, prime ministers, and presidents on my journey.

Everything God has promised me has come to pass. God answers prayer; He doesn't require that you see Him, only that He sees you. Wherever you are, in whatever trouble you may find yourself, you are free to call upon

Him in prayer. The story of the shepherd/king is one of a man's face bronzed by the blazing heat of adversity. He faced a giant and a demon-driven king. He was elevated by Jehovah to become the most famous king in Israel. David had a heart filled with delight in a holy God. His fingerprints and the record of his extravagant love affair with the God of Israel are imprinted in the pages of the Old Testament. David's life was not without sin; he committed adultery and even murder. Yet it was failure that drew him to God. It was his passion to touch God in prayer, and his hungry heart that activated a heavenly response. David prayed with a voracious desperation, knowing prayer was his only avenue to Jehovah. God took David's broken heart and from its depths inspired him to write: "He that dwelleth in the secret place of the most High shall abide under the shadow of the Almighty. I will say of the Lord, He is my refuge and my fortress: my God; in him will I trust" (Psalm 91:1–2 kjv).

David had learned that lesson as a shepherd. God had miraculously provided protection for him and for his flock. When David faced the giant, he was prepared. Crossing the brook, David selected five smooth stones and dropped them into his shepherd's bag.

As he approached the Valley of Elah, Goliath began to fling insults:

> He said to David, "Am I a dog, that you come at me with sticks?" And the Philistine cursed David by his gods. "Come here," he said, "and I'll give your flesh to the birds and the wild animals!" (1 Samuel 17:43–44 NIV)

David's battle cry was simply: "I come against you in the name of the Lord Almighty, the God of the armies of Israel, whom you have defied" (1 Samuel 17:45b NIV).

God had proven to be strong in battle, present during trials, Light in the darkness, Living Water in the desert, David's Provider. That was the basis for David's humility, knowing that he himself could do nothing but that he could do anything through God if his faith was rooted and grounded in Him.

In the end, Goliath lay on the ground—one of David's five stones that he had secreted in his pouch embedded deeply in the giant's forehead. David then used the giant's own weapon to lop off his head and give Israel the victory—not by might, nor by power, but by the Spirit of the Lord of hosts (see Zechariah 4:6, paraphrased). David had long known that with God on his side, he was in the majority.

I have had baggage in my life, especially as an abused child. The Holy Spirit has taught me that God can turn a broken heart into art, grief into glory, and pain into power, purpose, and passion. God touched David in a way that changed his world forever. He did the same for me, as you will see in the pages of this book. Once He did, my world was never the same, and neither will yours be.

Psalm 37:23–24 reads: "The steps of a good man are ordered by the LORD; and he delighteth in his way. Though he fall, he shall not be utterly cast down: for the LORD upholdeth him with his hand" (KJV).

As with King David, I live each day expecting a miracle. God is ready to anoint what you have. David was able to defeat the enemy of his soul because he allowed God to define who and what he was. I, too, remain ready for another outpouring of that anointing in my life. Like David, I pray with a desperate and hungry heart. David knew, as I know, that prayer is the only way.

The New Testament begins with Jesus Christ, the descendant of the king of Judah; it ends with: "I am the Root and the Offspring of David, the Bright and Morning Star" (Revelation 22:16 NKJV).

God gave David—and me—a future and a hope; He will give you the same. God gave David the means to a bright future and a throne. Do not let past experiences hold you back. David could have declared he was but a shepherd boy unfit to rule an entire nation. I could have used my lack of relationship with an abusive father to keep me from reaching my God-ordained goals. The prophet Jeremiah wrote in chapter 29, verses 11–13 (NKJV):

> For I know the thoughts that I think toward you, says the Lord, thoughts of peace and not of evil, to give you a future and a hope. Then you will call upon Me and go and pray to Me, and I will listen to you. And you will seek Me and find Me, when you search for Me with all your heart.

David had both drive and determination. He was resolved that nothing would hinder him from the call God had placed on his life. He would battle giants, elude the armies of kings, or whatever it took to reach the promised throne. I, too, made a commitment to God to answer His call. For the life of my ministry, He has opened doors that seemed impossible to open. The days, weeks, months, and years that have raced by have been invested in His kingdom. As a child, I was "afraid of the rats"; I have come to realize that when you and I are armed with the Word of Truth, nothing is impossible.

SCRIPTURES ON FEAR AND ANXIETY

Isaiah 41:10—Fear thou not; for I am with thee: be not dismayed; for I am thy God: I will strengthen thee; yea, I will help thee; yea, I will uphold thee with the right hand of my righteousness.

Philippians 4:6–7—Be careful for nothing; but in every thing by prayer and supplication with thanksgiving let your requests be made known unto God.

Psalm 56:3—What time I am afraid, I will trust in thee.

2 Timothy 1:7—For God hath not given us the spirit of fear; but of power, and of love, and of a sound mind.

Deuteronomy 31:6—Be strong and of a good courage, fear not, nor be afraid of them: for the Lord thy God, he it is that doth go with thee; he will not fail thee, nor forsake thee.

Psalm 34:4—I sought the Lord, and he heard me, and delivered me from all my fears.

1 Peter 5:7—Casting all your care upon him; for he careth for you.

1 John 4:18—There is no fear in love; but perfect love casteth out fear: because fear hath torment. He that feareth is not made perfect in love.

Isaiah 35:4—Say to them that are of a fearful heart, Be strong, fear not: behold, your God will come with vengeance, even God with a recompence; he will come and save you.

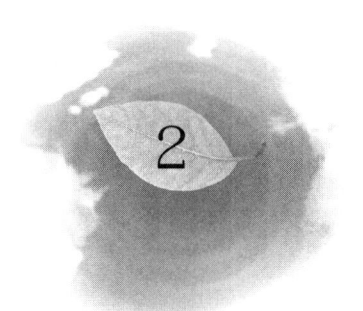

I DON'T WANT TO FEED THE PIGEONS!

(FEELING EMPTY AND WANTING MORE)

My earliest recollection of abuse in my home was at the age of four. Something had set off my dad one morning; he was stomping around the house yelling and screaming at my mother, calling her a "whore." He took a swing at her, and when she fell to the floor, it terrified me. I ran from the house and raced several blocks down the sidewalk to the local park. I had gone there often with my older sister Sherry.

It was October and the leaves in New England were changing color. On cold, bare feet I sprinted down the street, sobs bursting from my throat and tears coursing down my cheeks. I was panicked by the thought that I could hear the heavy thud of my father's boots following me. I neared the entrance to the park and glanced over my shoulder but saw no one. As I turned back, I ran headlong into a group of senior citizens, who I later discovered were on an outing to the park from a local nursing home. It was an opportunity for them to visit, do a little bird-watching, and feed the pigeons in the park.

A nurse accompanying the group reached out to keep me from falling. "Hi, little guy! Are you running from the bogeyman? Don't worry; you're safe here with us."

She took out her handkerchief and dried my face, and then she offered bread crumbs to me. "Do you want to help me feed the pigeons?"

I was still so scared my father would come after me that I pulled away and screamed, "I don't want to feed the stupid pigeons!" Somehow I sensed, even at that early age, there had to be more in life for me.

I knocked the bread crumbs away, whirled, and ran down the sidewalk toward the street. At the end of the sidewalk, I saw the flashing lights of a police car. Surprisingly, my sister Sherry was inside. Standing outside were two police officers. As she tried to convince me to go home, I kept screaming, "No, he'll hit me." She tried to protect Dad by telling the officers that our mom had fallen when Dad reached out to help her. She said I thought Dad had hit Mom, and it scared me. Sherry finally convinced me to ride home with her in the police car, but not before one of the officers had slipped me a piece of peppermint candy to help soothe my fear.

All the way home, Sherry kept repeating that Mom had slipped and fallen. I was equally certain that Dad had hit her, but my four-year-old mind was focused on the piece of peppermint candy I clutched in my hand.

I've often wondered if God put those precious old people in my pathway that day to keep me from harm, from perhaps falling into the nearby pond. Of course, at the time, I didn't know the Bible said, "For He shall give His angels charge over you, to keep you in all your ways" (Psalm 91:11 NKJV). Years later I have been able to look back at my life and see the ways God has kept me from death and destruction. Perhaps you can think of such times in your own life.

From that moment forward, I felt emptiness inside that could not be assuaged by peppermint candy or assurances from my sister. As the years passed, I would discover from my own experiences that my father was, indeed, an angry and abusive man. The emptiness grew; I wanted more in my small world—affection, affirmation, and accord—but was not sure how to attain what I needed.

Are you in the same situation? Perhaps from abuse, illness, broken relationships, or other equally devastating circumstances? The author of Acts wrote:

> "For in Him we live and move and have our being, as also some of your own poets have said, 'For we are also His offspring.'" (Acts 17:28 NKJV)

What joyful news! "In Him we live." Our heavenly Father holds us in His loving but powerful hand. Isaiah proclaimed, "Behold, I have engraved you on the palms of my hands" (Isaiah 49:16 ESV). Your name is written in the palm of God's hand. You have no idea how much God loves you. He has loved you from the beginning of time. You can't earn His love; you can only receive what He freely offers. He carries a picture of you—not in His wallet but engraved on the palm of His hand! He created you for love and fellowship, but that cannot come unless you open your heart to Him. He will use every fragment of your broken life for good.

Paul reminds us in 1 Corinthians 6:20 (NLT), "For God bought you with a high price." We are His dearly loved offspring. John, the Beloved, penned, "For God so loved the world that He gave His only begotten Son, that whoever believes in Him should not perish but have everlasting life" (John 3:16 NKJV).

God loves you so much that He wants to fill all the empty places in your life with His presence. Too many seek to fill those empty places with everything *but* God. Men often depend on their jobs, their wives or lovers, toys—boats, cars, electronic gadgets—drugs, or alcohol to fill the empty places. The truth is: There is a God-sized vacuum in the spirit of Man and nothing can fill it except the Creator. God's love at work in our lives confers so many benefits upon us. Because of His great love, we feel cherished.

Self-worth: As a child, I had no sense of self-worth. I saw myself through the eyes of my earthly father who, more often than not, called me "moron."

Victims of abuse—physical or psychological—instinctively perceive their self-worth to be under attack. This causes deep wounds to the self-esteem of its victims; they are hindered in forming healthy relationships. Someone who has experienced success may, as the writer of Romans 12:3 warned, "Think of himself more highly than he ought" (KJV). Conversely, an individual who has suffered constant verbal and/or physical abuse may feel totally worthless and incapable of achieving any success in life. That's the way it had been with me year after year. The first link of the tormentor's chain around my neck had been forged in the fires of my father's hatred; it was the link of bitterness, along with a sickening sense of hopelessness and defeat because I had no self-worth. Wonderful opportunities and successes were coming to me in the ministry, but my sense of unworthiness and fear of failure kept me from enjoying them.

If you and I are to experience healing and wholeness, our self-perception must be reshaped from one who has been devalued to one who senses his great worth in the sight of God. But to reach that goal, we need more than a strong will and faith in ourselves. We need God to take us by the hand and walk us through the rough places, as well as the smooth places. We need a heavenly Father to encourage us, instill confidence and a sense of self-worth in us, and believe in us.

The emptiness of insecurity can be filled when we accept God's love. Satan will use any chink in our armor—any weakness—to hit us with a fiery dart. This seems especially true when a child is the victim of abuse. Emotional abandonment—the lack of love and nurturing—is devastating. Rejection leads to insecurity. Those past hurts can cause an emotional logjam that only God can untangle. John 8:36 reminds us, "Therefore if the Son makes you free, you shall be free indeed" (NKJV).

The "Father of Lies" stands ready to turn even the most innocent conversation or encounter into an attack of insecurity. We begin to question our motives, our attitudes, our own veracity in an onslaught of lies and half-truths. As we do, the Enemy comes in like a flood and wreaks havoc on our imagination. (See 2 Corinthians 10:5)

The end result is a veritable loop of lies, imagination, insecurity, and depression. It is the counterpart of spiritual "death by a thousand cuts," the equivalent of *lingchi*, "a highly unpleasant form of execution used in Imperial China, which involved the slicing of the. . . flesh until death ensued."[3] Without the sure cure for insecurity, the price to be paid is high, indeed—mental and emotional instability, a turning away from the only One who can effect a cure. The elixir can be found in 2 Corinthians 10:4–5 (KJV):

> (For the weapons of our warfare are not carnal, but mighty through God to the pulling down of strong holds;) Casting down imaginations, and every high thing that exalteth itself against the knowledge of God, and bringing into captivity every thought to the obedience of Christ.

When we realize that we are "accepted in the Beloved," (Ephesians 1:6 NKJV), the bonds can be broken, and the misery of insecurity will be mended. As Isaiah promised in chapter 62, verse 4, you will have a new name: "But you shall be called Hephzibah [my delight is in her]."

Why are self-worth and security important in the life of a Believer? If one's self-worth is shattered, if the child of God is insecure, he/she will hesitate to step out in faith to do whatever God has called them to do. Fear of failure becomes a debilitating force. Crosswalk.com contributor Whitney Hopler wrote:

> Understand that security can only be found in the peace God offers you through Jesus. Embrace your identity as God's beloved child and be assured that, through your relationship with Jesus, you have all the power you need to do God's will in every situation.[4]

Once we are secure in the love of God, once we are strong in the Lord and in the power of His might, we can stand against principalities and powers (see Ephesians 6). No longer do we have to plod through life feeling empty and wanting more; we will have Him! We are assured that He neither slumbers nor sleeps; God watches over His children. That has been made obvious to me again and again.

In October 1982, a member of my ministry team and I were on our way home in a private plane piloted by a friend, Bill Knight. Paul Cole and I had just completed taping a television special, *Israel, America's Key to Survival*. As we neared our destination, the engine malfunctioned, and we could smell the fuel that was spewing from the engine; the lights on the instrument panel had gone out, and we were flying blind in a dark sky. I asked Bill what was happening, and he replied that the engine was breaking apart. He added that we were twenty-five minutes from Waco, but he could not land the plane without lights. He said we had a fifty mile-per-hour headwind that was preventing the engine from catching fire.

When he uttered those words, I could envision my obituary in the *Fort Worth Star Telegram*. I rebuked the Destroyer and began to pray, "Angels of the Lord, undergird us. . . angels of the Lord, undergird us."

Twenty-one minutes later the pilot glided to a landing at the airport in Waco. When he checked over the plane, we were astonished to learn that an engine mount had broken loose, and the engine was totally drained of oil. We had truly experienced the power and presence of God on that flight—a miracle. The following morning a ministry partner, Opal Weeks, had called the office and reported to my secretary that the night before she had been awakened from sleep and impressed to pray that the Lord would undergird Brother Mike wherever he was. All she could pray for thirty minutes was "Angels of the Lord, undergird Mike; angels of the Lord, undergird Mike." She said at 11:55 p.m. the burden lifted. That was the exact time we had landed in Waco. What Satan meant for evil on that dark and starless night, God turned to good.

The story is told of an early American Indian tribe with a unique method of transitioning their youngsters from that of childhood to brave. After thirteen years of training in every aspect of becoming a warrior—hunting, scouting, riding, and survival in the wilderness—the young man would spend an entire night alone in the forest, away from the scrutiny and security of his tribal family. On the night in question, he would be blindfolded and led deep into the dark woods several miles from the village.

When he removed the blindfold, he would find himself alone in the black night, surrounded by strange sounds. Each time a twig snapped, he might have imagined a dangerous animal stalking him. After what seemed like an eternal, sleepless night, the first rays of sunlight penetrated the forest. Looking around, the boy spotted the path that would lead him to safety. As he started forward, he was utterly amazed to find his father, armed with a bow and arrow, sitting near a tree a few feet away. The father had been keeping watch all night long.[5]

Each time God provides a way of escape for His children, it is a time for rejoicing and confidence building. God is the path of protection; no matter the situation or circumstance, our heavenly Father is there to walk through it with us. You and I are never alone. He has promised that He will never leave or forsake His children.

SCRIPTURES ON GOD'S PROVISION

2 Corinthians 9:8—And God is able to make all grace abound toward you; that ye, always having all sufficiency in all things, may abound to every good work:

Philippians 4:19—But my God shall supply all your need according to his riches in glory by Christ Jesus.

Psalm 37:25–26—I have been young, and now am old; yet have I not seen the righteous forsaken, nor his seed begging bread.

Philippians 4:11–12—Not that I speak in respect of want: for I have learned, in whatsoever state I am, therewith to be content.

Deuteronomy 28:1–68—And it shall come to pass, if thou shalt hearken diligently unto the voice of the Lord thy God, to observe and to do all his commandments which I command thee this day, that the Lord thy God will set thee on high above all nations of the earth:

1 Timothy 5:8—But if any provide not for his own, and specially for those of his own house, he hath denied the faith, and is worse than an infidel.

Psalm 46:1—(To the chief Musician for the sons of Korah, A Song upon Alamoth.) God is our refuge and strength, a very present help in trouble.

Matthew 6:33—But seek ye first the kingdom of God, and his righteousness; and all these things shall be added unto you.

3

YOU'RE A GOOD BOY

(GOD WILL NOT FORSAKE YOU)

Each morning as I made my way to Indian Orchard Elementary School, I encountered a lady who can only be described as an angel in disguise. Mrs. Panelli was the crossing guard. When she raised her hand, traffic stopped so that we could safely make our way from one side of the street to the other. With a yellow vest securely fastened over her clothing, she was the symbol of authority—but always with a smile and a word of encouragement.

When I was in second grade, Mrs. Panelli made a proclamation that I have never forgotten. She smiled at me and said, "Michael, you're a good boy. Someday you will be a preacher." She likely had no idea that she had prophesied over my life. Her statement hovered on the edge of my consciousness until it came to pass after I entered Bible school near Fort Worth, Texas.

Before that came to pass, however, I had learned what it was to work and help provide for my siblings. At age eleven, I harvested tobacco with Mexican migrant workers. We would be picked up about 4:30 a.m. in a closed-panel truck and taken to the tobacco fields. By the age of fifteen, I worked three jobs: construction, bagging groceries, and waxing floors all night on Fridays and Saturdays. I'd long since given up attending high school to work full time. When I received my paycheck, it was like Christmas for the kids at home; I would buy gifts for them.

My friend Jim and I tried to enlist in the Army at the age of sixteen. I had attempted to join the Marines but failed to pass the physical. The army recruiter, however, was delighted to see us and administered an aptitude test during our first visit. I mistakenly thought I could pass by checking off all "A" answers on the first page; "B" answers on the second page, and "C" answers on the third. Somehow, though, I managed to achieve a passing score on the written portion. Passing the physical exam proved more problematic.

Although I was tall for my age, I still was thin and terribly underweight because of a stomach issue. I'd been eating much better since the stomach pain was gone, but my overall size hadn't caught up with my height. When the recruiter weighed me he glanced down at the scale and shook his head. "Boy, you're too skinny. For your height, you need to weigh at least one hundred thirty-two pounds."

I was crushed, and I like to think he was disappointed, too. Jim and I were eager young men nearing prime military age. The recruiter seemed as eager to have us as we were to join. Still, rules were rules.

"Go home and try eating bananas," he suggested finally. "Maybe that'll fatten you up enough to get you into the army."

The suggestion sounded strange. I had never heard of eating bananas as a way of gaining weight but I was intent on enlisting and did as I was told. For weeks after that I ate bananas every day—as many as my stomach could tolerate. Though I stuffed myself with that and everything else I could hold, I failed to gain an ounce. Day after day I stepped onto the scale at the drug store, only to look down and see the needle stuck on 111.

Determined to solve the weight problem, I decided to resort to other measures and made a trip uptown to Ryan's Sporting Goods. After looking through the store's shelves, I located five-pound weights that appeared useable and bought four of them. Later, at home, I devised a method of strapping the weights to my thighs using a couple of belts.

Later that week, I returned to the recruiter's office with the weights in place. I was worried they would slip down my legs and took small steps in an attempt to prevent that from happening. It felt awkward—and I'm sure it looked awkward, too—but I made it through the initial interview, and when the recruiter told me to strip to my shorts, I stepped into the restroom and adjusted the weights just to be sure.

Wearing nothing but boxer shorts, I walked back to the room and, sure enough, the weights shifted on my legs—only the shift was toward the inside. Pain shot through my body and I was on the verge of tears—both from the physical trauma and the angst of being discovered—but no one seemed to notice my predicament. Covertly glancing from side to side, I continued across the room and stepped onto the scale.

"Boy," the recruiter said with a grin, "I can't believe that banana trick really worked! You are exactly one hundred thirty-two pounds."

I stepped off the scale as quickly as possible, afraid he might change his mind. Then he patted me on the back and said, "You're in, but you're too young."

"Too young? I'm sixteen."

"Yeah," he replied, "but you have to be seventeen years

old to sign up on your own. Otherwise, you need your parents' consent. Come back on your seventeenth birthday and we'll send you off for Basic. You'll be in the army."

That was one of the proudest days of my life. I was going into the army! After I dressed, I asked about getting my parents' permission to join right then. The recruiter gave me a form and said, "Tell me, do you have any idea where you'd like to be stationed?"

A map was posted on the wall of the office. I studied it a moment, trying to determine the point farthest from Springfield. Pushpins marked the location of places where US troops were stationed. "There," I said, pointing to a spot in South Korea. "I want to be stationed right there."

Although the Korean War had officially ended in 1953, the United States still had troops stationed in South Korea along the demilitarized zone to deter the North Koreans from slipping across the border. As best I could tell, it was the farthest point on the map from Springfield and the farthest away from my father.

I pointed again at the map, "There. I want to go to South Korea."

"Good," he nodded. "We'll see what we can do about that."

On Thanksgiving Day while Dad was eating turkey and watching the parades, I slipped up beside him, held out the enlistment papers, and asked, "Dad, would you sign this so a recruiter can come by and talk to you about me going into the army?" He downed a couple of goofballs with a swig of Jack Daniel's and laughed uproariously, "You'll never make it. They don't take morons!" He snatched the papers out of my hand and signed them. They were not consent for a recruiter to visit; he had signed the form giving his permission for me to join. I later discovered that he could actually read very little.

I took the military enlistment oath and was soon shipped to boot camp. As I walked from the house, instead of wishing me well, Dad stood on the porch screaming, "You're garbage, you #@$% moron! You'll be in the stockade in six months."

During my tour in the army, I was sent to South Korea. After I completed my tour of duty there, I returned to the States and was assigned to a recruiting post in Philadelphia. It was in the "City of Brotherly Love" that I was robbed of all my belongings—clothes, wallet, and vehicle. The only thing I could find to get off the streets was a bed at the Salvation Army. After several nights there, I received my army pay and was able to rent a room at a local YMCA.

Night after night in my sparsely furnished room, I would close myself in with God, praying and searching the Scriptures. Someone once said, "A Bible that is falling apart usually belongs to a person who isn't." I drank only water that week as I beseeched God in prayer. I pointed to a battered chair in the corner and prayed, "Jesus, You came to me when I was eleven; this is Your chair. Please come back, sit and talk with me; I am ready to listen and obey." As I fasted and prayed, I read through the entire New Testament.

It was during that time I felt what can only be described as a force compelling me to attend a Bible college near Fort Worth in order to prepare myself for the ministry. Although I had not completed high school, I did have a GED that I had obtained while in Korea and was certain Bible school was what God intended me to pursue. For the next two years I spent most nights in the dormitory prayer room desperately seeking God's plan and purpose for my life.

I knew that God had not forsaken me; His presence was very real as I made the transition from military service to God's army. It was very apparent to me that I had nothing without God; He held my present and future in the palm of His hand.

When we reach that place in our lives, it is humbling to realize that He is the only One you and I can trust unconditionally. God says to us: "I will never leave you nor forsake you" (Hebrews 13:5b NKJV). When asked the secret of life, we can reply confidently, "Trust in God and no other."

For those who have been betrayed or abandoned by a parent, a spouse, a friend, it may be difficult to comprehend that kind of trust—one that will never be betrayed. When we grasp that promise, when we allow it to sink deeply into our spirit, you and I will be transformed.

Looking back at the moment the decision was made to attend Bible school, I was bereft of everything—car, clothing, funds. Nothing else mattered; only God. It is then, when we reach that point, that God can teach us the lesson of trust. There are countless examples through the Bible of men and women who learned that lesson. Perhaps one of the most important is that God will not forsake His children.

When the People of the Book had been led forth from Egypt by Moses, had been saved by passing through the Red Sea, and had seen God's miraculous provision in the desert of manna, quail, and water from a rock, you would think that they knew God well. In fact they still refused to draw near to Him, still refused to fully trust Him. Even though they had seen Moses ascend the mountain and come back unharmed, his face glowing with the glory of the Lord, they chose to have someone else between them and God at all times because they feared knowing God personally.

In other words, though they knew of God's greatness, of His miracle-working power to deliver, and had heard Him speak from the cloud and the mountaintop, they still did not want to get too close to Him. They said, "Go *thou* near"—in other words, "Moses, *you* go and talk to God. *You* go and find out His plans. Then come tell us. We will do whatever He wants, but we just don't want to have to get that close to Him."

The first day God supplied manna for the Israelites, He gave specific instructions for gathering it. In Exodus 16 (4–5 NKJV), we read:

> Then the LORD said to Moses, "Behold, I will rain bread from heaven for you. And the people shall go out and gather a certain quota every day, that I may test them, whether they will walk in My law or not. And it shall be on the sixth day that they shall prepare what they bring in, and it shall be twice as much as they gather daily."

The Israelites were to gather only enough manna for one day for family members—no more, no less. That was an exercise in trust. The children of Israel had to learn that Jehovah would supply their needs one day at a time, except immediately before the Sabbath when He would provide food sufficient for two days. Of course, there were those who waivered. The Bible records:

> So the people of Israel went out and gathered it—some getting more and some less before it melted on the ground, and there was just enough for everyone. Those who gathered more had nothing left over and those who gathered little had no lack! Each home had just enough. And Moses told them, "Don't leave it overnight." But of course some of them wouldn't listen, and left it until morning; and when they looked, it was full of maggots and had a terrible odor; and Moses was very angry with them. (Exodus 16:17–20 TLB)

The pages of Scripture are rife with examples of a lack of trust—the rich young ruler, Ananias and his wife, Sapphira, Moses, Saul, and more. Conversely, there were others who trusted that God would not forsake them: David, Noah, Joseph, Rahab, Ruth, and many others.

Of course, the provision of manna for the Israelites was mirrored by Elijah's miracle of oil and flour. Elijah had placed his very life in God's hands. He submitted to the command to go to Zarephath immediately without question or hesitation. When the drought worsened and the brook dried up, God sent the prophet on a long, dangerous walk from his cave all the way to the Mediterranean coast and the home of a widow and her only son. Elijah asked the woman for bread and water. Her answer must have stunned the prophet:

> "As surely as the Lord your God lives," she replied, "I don't have any bread—only a handful of flour in a jar and a little olive oil in a jug. I am gathering a few sticks to take home and make a meal for myself and my son, that we may eat it—and die." (1 Kings 17:12 NIV)

Jehovah breathed the solution into Elijah's spirit:

> Elijah said to her, "Don't be afraid. Go home and do as you have said. But first make a small loaf of bread for me from what you

have and bring it to me, and then make something for yourself and your son." (1 Kings 17:13 NIV)

That instruction must have been humbling—the great prophet of God sent to eat a piece of flatbread from the last smidgen of flour and oil the widow possessed. Elijah was not to give; he was to take—and trust the provision of Jehovah. As a prophet of God accustomed to the miraculous, he surely must have wanted to be the one to provide an abundant supply for this widow—a room filled with oil, flour, lentils, vegetables—but no. As He had with the children of Israel who received manna sufficient for the day, God supplied a daily quantity of flour and oil for the widow, her son, and their houseguest. She had trusted God for provision; Jehovah-Jireh—the God who provides—answered.

Because the widow offered Elijah the last of her food, God miraculously supplied her needs:

> The bin of flour was not used up, nor did the jar of oil run dry, according to the word of the Lord which He spoke by Elijah. (1 Kings 17:16 NKJV)

A former Methodist pastor, Rev. Dr. Allen Hunt wrote:

> Place your hope solely in God. When you do, you will thereby discover life, true life. Not from money, not from people but from him and no place else. When you grasp this one simple promise, your life truly will be different because hope and life can be found nowhere else.[6]

Daniel and his friends Shadrach, Meshach, and Abednego had the promise of God's presence even before they were taken captive and marched from their homeland to Babylon. These four young men had cut their teeth on the laws of God, specifically the Ten Commandments. Moses had instructed the children of Israel in Deuteronomy 11:19 that the Word of Jehovah was to be taught to the children "when you sit in your house, when you walk by the way, when you lie down, and when you rise up" (NKJV). The tenets and precepts of God's law were ingrained in the minds and spirits of those young men.

The first and second commandments are very specific:

> "You shall have no other gods before me. You shall not make for yourself an image in

the form of anything in heaven above or on the earth beneath or in the waters below. You shall not bow down to them or worship them... (Exodus 20:3–5a NIV)

The day appointed by Nebuchadnezzar arrived accompanied by great pomp and ceremony. Off to one side of the dais from which the king held court was a reminder of the punishment for disobedience: the ovens into which those who refused to bow would be thrown. On the plain surrounding the image, the people gathered in anticipation of the musical strains that were to signal the moment to fall on their faces and worship the golden statue.

The powers of darkness danced in anticipation of the destruction of the trio of Hebrews in the king's court who were unlikely to bow. Satan probably waited with sulfurous breath to see the defeat of God's chosen people. The king had decreed compliance with his edict; God declared a different scenario. When Nebuchadnezzar looked out over the prostrate participants, he saw three young men standing tall—Shadrach, Meshach, and Abednego. They had determined not to disgrace the God of heaven. Jehovah was their Lord and King—they would bow to no other.

Their detractors—those jealous of the honors that had been bestowed on Daniel and his companions—could not wait to advise the king that three of his subjects had dared to flagrantly defy his order:

> "But there are some Jews whom you have set over the affairs of the province of Babylon—Shadrach, Meshach and Abednego—who pay no attention to you, Your Majesty. They neither serve your gods nor worship the image of gold you have set up." (Daniel 3:12 NIV)

Nebuchadnezzar's anger boiled. How dare they not obey his commandment! He ordered the men brought to stand in his presence. He demanded, "Is it true? Did you not bow down before the golden image as I ordered? Don't you know the punishment that awaits you if you refuse to bow?"

Shadrach, Meshach, and Abednego quietly explained to the king that they could not bow to any image because of their fidelity to Jehovah God. Nebuchadnezzar's visage grew darker as he pointed toward the ovens burning brightly in the distance. He ordered the instruments to play again in order to give these three young men a second chance to adhere to his instructions. Again they refused. As they stood before the king, the three Hebrew men replied:

> "King Nebuchadnezzar, we do not need to defend ourselves before you in this matter. If we are thrown into the blazing furnace, the God we serve is able to deliver us from it, and he will deliver us from Your Majesty's hand. But even if he does not, we want you to know, Your Majesty, that we will not serve your gods or worship the image of gold you have set up." (Daniel 3:16–18 NIV)

The king was infuriated by their answer. He ordered the ovens stoked seven times hotter. He then commanded the mightiest men in his army to bind the trio and toss them into the furnace. So hot was the fire that the men who marched Shadrach, Meshach, and Abednego to the furnace were killed. As the young men who stood strong in His Name landed in the midst of the fire, God poured out His favor upon them and joined them there. As the fire lapped up the bindings of His servants, Jehovah tamed the flames—they lost the ability to devour.

From his royal perch high above the furnace, the king watched in anticipation of seeing the three defiant Hebrews totally destroyed. Suddenly, his triumph turned to fear. He grew pale as he lurched from the throne and pointed toward the all-consuming flames. He stuttered, "Did we not cast three men bound into the midst of the fire? . . . Look! . . . I see four men loose, walking in the midst of the fire; and they are not hurt, and the form of the fourth is like the Son of God" (Daniel 3:24, 25 NKJV).

In amazement, the king abandoned his throne and strode across the plain, royal robes flying behind him. He crept as close to the fire as he safely could and cried:

> "Shadrach, Meshach and Abed-Nego, servants of the Most High God, come out, and come here." Then Shadrach, Meshach, and Abed-Nego came from the midst of the fire. And the satraps, administrators, governors, and the king's counselors gathered together, and they saw these men on whose bodies the fire had no power; the hair of their head was not singed nor were their garments affected, and the smell of fire was not on them. (Daniel 3:26–27 NKJV)

Nebuchadnezzar was overwhelmed by the miracle of the power and presence of the God that Shadrach, Meshach, and Abednego served.

Jehovah doesn't want us to place our trust in *things*. When I checked in to a room at the YMCA, I had nothing left but the clothes on my back. My custom-made suits from South Korea—gone. My car—gone. My wallet—gone. God—still there! He had never left nor forsaken me. The lesson: He was more than enough and would supply my needs according to His riches in glory by Christ Jesus (see Philippians 4:19).

It is not what you have; I didn't have anything. It's not who you know; I didn't know anyone important at the time. If we place our trust in Him, we have the promise of His presence. We need nothing more.

SCRIPTURES ON GOD'S PLAN FOR YOU

Jeremiah 29:11—For I know the thoughts that I think toward you, saith the Lord, thoughts of peace, and not of evil, to give you an expected end.

Proverbs 16:9—A man's heart deviseth his way: but the Lord directeth his steps.

Proverbs 19:21—There are many devices in a man's heart; nevertheless the counsel of the Lord, that shall stand.

Matthew 6:25–34—Therefore I say unto you, Take no thought for your life, what ye shall eat, or what ye shall drink; nor yet for your body, what ye shall put on. Is not the life more than meat, and the body than raiment?

Ephesians 2:10—For we are his workmanship, created in Christ Jesus unto good works, which God hath before ordained that we should walk in them.

Jeremiah 1:5—Before I formed thee in the belly I knew thee; and before thou camest forth out of the womb I sanctified thee, and I ordained thee a prophet unto the nations.

1 John 5:4—For whatsoever is born of God overcometh the world: and this is the victory that overcometh the world, even our faith.

Psalm 138:8—The Lord will perfect that which concerneth me: thy mercy, O Lord, endureth for ever: forsake not the works of thine own hands.

4

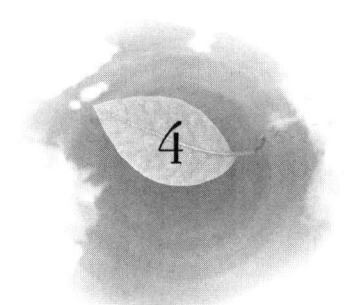

"BILLY GRAHAM, THE POPE, AND ADOLF HITLER ARE ALL CHRISTIANS"

(NO MATTER WHAT YOU ARE GOING THROUGH, GOD CREATED YOU FOR A PURPOSE)

One Saturday morning, I was sprawled in front of the television set in the living room watching cartoons. When the last program ended, my attention wandered. The next thing I knew, my mother had run into the room and snapped off the set. "Michael," she shouted as she shook her finger at the screen, "don't ever let me catch you watching this again! Billy Graham, the Pope, and Adolf Hitler are all Christians. Christians hate Jews; Christians kill Jews! Jesus died; don't dig Him up."

Her anger stemmed from the fact that most of her family members had died in Nazi concentration camps during the Holocaust. During those years of terror and suffering, her grandfather, Rabbi Mikael Katznelson, had succumbed in his synagogue. In Vishnyeva, in the heart of White Russia, the Nazis used a different technique to eliminate Jews. They didn't shoot them; they burned them alive. The Nazis and Russian Orthodox locals rounded up all the Jews remaining in the hamlet. Men, women, and children were then forced to march to the synagogue, which was made of wood. They were herded inside the building, the windows and doors were nailed shut, and the place of worship was set aflame. Two thousand Jews died in that fire as those gathered outside screamed, "Christ killers!" That rabbi was my great-grandfather; the synagogue's rabbi cantor, Zvi Meltzer, was the grandfather of former Israeli president and prime minister, the late Shimon Peres—my good friend.

I'm not sure when my mother learned of what happened to Mikael, his wife, Goldy, and the people of Vishnyeva, but from what she said about events there, I believe news of their death reached her during the war. Certainly long before any of her children were born. She first told me about it when I was still a young boy, and the way she did it that Saturday morning had made a lasting impression on me.

It is difficult sometimes, especially in the midst of chaos, to understand that you and I were created for a purpose and then to discover what it is. Like a good dream that doesn't last until morning, personal peace is fleeting, and achieving a fulfilling purpose for living eludes us. We seem to be a nation of people who, while struggling to know our divine destiny, settle for complacency.

There are numerous examples in the pages of Scripture of men and women who began life in obscurity but were raised up to positions of prominence—David, Ruth, Esther, Joseph, and Gideon among them. These men and women were born with a purpose, and in due time God revealed it to them. They received supernatural favor from kings, priests, generals, and wealthy landowners. Because of their submission to the will and purpose of God for their lives, David became a king, Esther a queen, Joseph a leader over all Egypt, Ruth an ancestor of our Lord, and Gideon a mighty warrior. Each overcame vastly different circumstances to enjoy the favor of both God and man.

Rev. Paul Aiello, Jr. shared an illustration about submission that has a valuable lesson for each of us:

> The captain of the ship looked into the
> dark night and saw faint lights in the distance.

Immediately he told his signalman to send a message: "Alter your course 10 degrees south."

Promptly a return message was received: "Alter your course 10 degrees north."

The captain was angered; his command had been ignored. So he sent a second message: "Alter your course 10 degrees south—I am the captain!"

Soon another message was received: "Alter your course 10 degrees north—I am seaman third class Jones."

Immediately the captain sent a third message, knowing the fear it would evoke: "Alter your course 10 degrees south—I am a battleship."

Then the reply came: "Alter your course 10 degrees north—I am a lighthouse."[7]

In the midst of our dark and foggy times, all sorts of voices are shouting orders into the night, telling us what to do, how to order our lives. Out of the darkness, one voice signals something quite opposite to the rest—something almost absurd. But the voice happens to be that of the Light of the World, and we ignore it at our peril. Heed that voice, and you and I are one step closer to finding our purpose in Him.

My ministry and travels have allowed me to meet many men and women of integrity. Shortly after the inauguration of President Ronald Reagan in 1985, I was invited to the White House for dinner with eighty-six religious leaders representing this nation. We were deeply moved by the warmth of the president. I was seated next to Chuck Colson. He had been special counsel to former President Richard Nixon and was making his first visit to the White House since Nixon's departure.

During the evening, I turned to Mr. Colson and said, "I imagine your mind is going a mile a minute thinking about the strategy of this meeting." He smiled and said, "No, quite the contrary. I'm going down to death row tonight to share Christ with prisoners who are scheduled to die, and my thoughts are on eternity." Integrity is not the absence of failure; it is the presence of God in the redeemed life.

Joseph's life, though one of integrity, had not been without failure, but God was able to teach him lessons about integrity and service that would prove invaluable during his stay in Egypt for the remainder of his life. As a young man, he was, perhaps, a bit egotistical and pretentious, a bit too eager to share his dreams with his jealous brothers. Even then, God had a plan and purpose for Joseph's life—one that would come to fruition only after overwhelming and demoralizing obstacles.

The Bible doesn't tell us how long or what humilities Joseph endured at the hands of the Ishmaelite traders after he was sold by his brothers. It is probable that his dirty face was lined with rivulets of tears that snaked their way from his eyes and dripped off his chin. It is also likely that he was subjected to indignity, deprivation, and flogging. He awoke one morning to find that the caravan of traders to which he had been sold had reached its destination—a slave market in Egypt, about to be sold once again to the highest bidder. Even so, God granted to him favor with a man from whom he should have had no hope of either mercy or grace.

It was on a very fortuitous day that Potiphar, the captain of the palace guard, was striding through the throngs of merchants in search of someone to take on the role of his personal household assistant. Something about Joseph captured the captain's attention. What was different about this young Hebrew? Was he standing to one side of the newly arrived batch of slaves watching as his traveling companions cursed and fought their captors? Did Joseph exude a quiet confidence not seen in the other human offerings? He was, after all, the offspring of Abraham, Isaac, and Jacob—men blessed by Jehovah—an incomparable heritage. Whatever they were, the things that attracted Potiphar to this young man resulted in Joseph being taken home to serve the captain. Genesis 39:2–4 (NKJV) relates:

> The Lord was with Joseph, and he was a successful man; and he was in the house of his master the Egyptian. And his master saw that the Lord was with him and that the Lord made all he did to prosper in his hand. So Joseph found favor in his sight, and served him.

God quickly endowed Joseph with favor so that he avoided some of the more harsh practices to which slaves were subjected, particularly that of castration. Joseph could have wallowed in "might have beens." Instead, he put his shoulder to the wheel and began a life of servitude that continued to win him favor. He walked with such integrity that Potiphar soon discovered Joseph could be trusted with everything in his house. Genesis 39:5–6 (NKJV) says:

> So it was, from the time that he had made him overseer of his house and all that he had,

> that the Lord blessed the Egyptian's house for Joseph's sake; and the blessing of the Lord was on all that he had in the house and in the field. Thus he left all that he had in Joseph's hand, and he did not know what he had except for the bread which he ate.

As the young Hebrew served his Egyptian master, Potiphar came to realize that even though he was not a servant of Yahweh—the Most High God—he was being blessed because of the presence of the son of Jacob. Joseph refused to take advantage of his master's trust, which likely did not win him friends among the other servants. This world could use more men like Joseph, who took his assignment seriously, worked hard, and lived a life of integrity no matter the price. How would you feel if your supervisor approached you to tell you what a blessing you, as a Christian, were to the organization?

Then, like the snake in the garden, Potiphar's wife reared her lustful head and tried repeatedly to seduce Joseph. He refused her advances and as a result life changed drastically for him. When Mrs. Potiphar (referred to in some Jewish commentaries as *Zuleika*) tried to drag Joseph into her snare, he fled leaving behind his cloak. He was once again left without a coat but was still clad in what Isaiah 61:10 says is the Believer's "garments of salvation," and a "robe of righteousness."

It is interesting to note that when his wife approached Potiphar and accused Joseph of assault, her husband didn't immediately have his slave put to death. Had he more trust in the integrity of Joseph than the veracity of his spouse? No, when you look at the scripture, you read, "Then Joseph's master took him and put him into the prison, a place where the king's prisoners were confined." Dr. David Albert Farmer, faculty member at Palmer Theological Seminary, wrote of Potiphar and his wife:

> One New Testament scholar points out that the prevailing law would have called for the death penalty as the proper punishment for attempted rape. This scholar suspects that Potiphar couldn't swallow his wife's tale hook, line, and sinker so he imprisoned the man he had trusted with his life and his wife, but he didn't have him put to death. He had to allow his wife to save face. Her lies easily could have gotten Joseph killed; that was of no concern to her. Only her wounded pride

and her unattended sexual desires mattered to her. What's the value of a Hebrew slave's life anyway? If you've read Dante's "Divine Comedy," which isn't funny at all, when the fictional Dante takes his tour of hell he sees Potiphar's wife. She is given no opportunity to speak by the writer, but another resident of hell tells Dante that with all other perjurers, she has been condemned to suffer a burning fever for all of eternity. . . . He is with symbols slamming all of those in history who have told lies, especially false accusations about innocent others—costing these innocents embarrassment, humiliation, job losses, and, yes, costing many of them their lives. Lies can kill.[8]

Once incarcerated, Joseph's sudden and unmerited fall from his owner's favor had no effect on Joseph's integrity. He continued to serve Yahweh and the keeper of the prison with equal reliability and soon had earned the trust of his overseers. Yes, Joseph had been falsely accused; and yes, he had been sentenced to prison. We know from Exodus 41:1 that he would have been hidden away in the depths of the dungeon before he saw the light of day again, but Joseph was unaware of what the future held for him. And although he had found favor with the warden, he was still a prisoner, with no revelation of what his purpose might be.

Shortly after being placed in the dungeon, Joseph had encounters with Pharaoh's chief baker and chief butler. Each man's sleep had been interrupted by a disturbing dream, which Joseph had interpreted. His only request was to be remembered by the butler when he was restored to his position in the palace. Three days later, the man was released, but it would be two long years before he thought again of the young Hebrew slave who had revealed the future to him.

Joseph, the son of Jacob's beloved wife, Rachel, the one for whom his father had designed a special coat of many colors, was in a seemingly purposeless place of suffering.

What Joseph—and indeed many of us—failed to realize is that even in the direst circumstances, God can and will turn our mourning into joy. Genesis 41:9–16 (NKJV) reveals how Joseph's life was about to change. The butler who had promised to remember his cellmate finally had an epiphany. He realized he had not fulfilled his promise to Joseph:

Then the chief butler spoke to Pharaoh, saying: "I remember my faults this day. When Pharaoh was angry with his servants, and put me in custody in the house of the captain of the guard, both me and the chief baker, we each had a dream in one night, he and I. Each of us dreamed according to the interpretation of his own dream. Now there was a young Hebrew man with us there, a servant of the captain of the guard. And we told him, and he interpreted our dreams for us; to each man he interpreted according to his own dream. And it came to pass, just as he interpreted for us, so it happened. He restored me to my office, and he hanged him." Then Pharaoh sent and called Joseph, and they brought him quickly out of the dungeon; and he shaved, changed his clothing, and came to Pharaoh. And Pharaoh said to Joseph, "I have had a dream, and there is no one who can interpret it. But I have heard it said of you that you can understand a dream, to interpret it." So Joseph answered Pharaoh, saying, "It is not in me; God will give Pharaoh an answer of peace."

On that fateful day, Joseph was going about his daily tasks—dirty, unshaven, clad in rags and totally unprepared for a divine encounter with Yahweh. He would soon find that God was setting the stage to reveal His purpose for Joseph's life. When summoned from the prison, imagine his reaction: Was Joseph about to be executed after all this time? Would he be freed only to be sold to a harsh taskmaster? As he responded to the call, he suddenly found that he was to be washed, shaved, and dressed in new garments. He must have been both stunned and confused. Following his spa-like treatment, Joseph was marched from the prison to the palace where he came face-to-face with Pharaoh, the undisputed ruler over all the land.

Joseph had no way of knowing that just the night before, Pharaoh had had a dream that left him unsettled. His magicians and mediums had failed to render a satisfactory interpretation, so he called for the man recommended by his butler. Joseph listened closely and then, giving all the credit and glory to Yahweh, revealed what was about to happen in the land: seven years of plenty unlike anything ever seen before, followed by seven years of drought that would decimate the land. He wanted Pharaoh to know that the King of Kings and Lord of Lords held the future of Egypt in His divine hand. Then Joseph advised Pharaoh:

> "Now therefore, let Pharaoh select a discerning and wise man, and set him over the land of Egypt. Let Pharaoh do this, and let him appoint officers over the land, to collect one-fifth of the produce of the land of Egypt in the seven plentiful years. And let them gather all the food of those good years that are coming, and store up grain under the authority of Pharaoh, and let them keep food in the cities. Then that food shall be as a reserve for the land for the seven years of famine which shall be in the land of Egypt, that the land may not perish during the famine." (Genesis 41:33–36 NKJV)

Guess who God had prepared to assume the role described and whose divine purpose was about to be revealed? It would be Joseph, the young man standing before him, and Pharaoh made his pronouncement in verse 39:

> "Inasmuch as God has shown you all this, there is no one as discerning and wise as you. You shall be over my house, and all my people shall be ruled according to your word; only in regard to the throne will I be greater than

you." And Pharaoh said to Joseph, "See, I have set you over all the land of Egypt." Then Pharaoh took his signet ring off his hand and put it on Joseph's hand; and he clothed him in garments of fine linen and put a gold chain around his neck.

Now, that's favor! Joseph had gone from having manacles around his wrists to Pharaoh's ring on his finger—a symbol of power, purpose, and prestige. Noted Christian writer Vance Havner wrote:

> God uses broken things. It takes broken soil to produce a crop, broken clouds to give rain, broken grain to give bread, broken bread to give strength. It is the broken alabaster box that gives forth perfume. It is Peter, weeping bitterly, who returns to greater power than ever.[9]

And, I might add, it took a broken and downcast Joseph to deliver his brethren—and an entire nation—from catastrophe. Joseph had no idea when he awoke that morning in a dank, dirty, and dark dungeon that before day's end he would be the second most important man in the realm—all because God had given him favor. Joseph's weeping had endured for a night, but the dawn brought joy and jubilation, peace, purpose, and promotion. As real as favor with God and man was for Joseph in the land of Egypt, so that same promise is available for the Believer today.

There were many women in the Bible who sought Jehovah's purpose with faith and integrity. One who exemplifies those traits is Ruth. This loving daughter-in-law was not afraid of hard work. This loving daughter-in-law was not afraid of hard work. Like the Proverbs 31 woman, Ruth rose while it was yet night and provided food (see verse 15) for herself and Naomi, her mother-in-law. Her faithfulness won favor with Boaz, led to their marriage, and gained Ruth a place in the genealogy of Jesus.

This was not a coincidence but the powerful hand of a loving Jehovah-Jireh who made provision for Ruth. It was the Holy Spirit who whispered into the ear of Boaz, *See that lovely and diligent young woman? Provide for her.* His obedience had kingdom consequences for a young woman who was just going about the business of taking care of a loved one, following the path and purpose God outlined for her.

As with Ruth, you and I are perhaps not meant to see the completed tapestry God is weaving in our lives, but we can make a difference by being faithful to the work of God.

It is He who provides purpose for our lives. Each of us has a purpose. We are not all called to lead nations or to produce an ancestor of Jesus Christ. For most, it is the common, everyday tasks that greet us when we arise.

For a loving breadwinner, it is getting up and going off to work to provide for his or her household.

For a dedicated parent, it is wiping runny noses and mopping up spilled milk.

For a pastor, it is serving the congregation in untold ways.

And God provides relief in just as many ways.

For the brokenhearted, it is trusting in your heavenly Father to give you hope.

For the suffering, it is reaching out to the One who can bind your wounds.

For the sinner, it is salvation and grace.

Every act of faithfulness, no matter how small, has the capacity to touch the life of someone. As God reveals your purpose in His kingdom, your trustworthiness can be used in a myriad of ways to bring glory to God.

Faithfulness equals obedience: simply doing what God's Word and the Holy Spirit instruct you and me to do. It is, again, listening to that still, small voice and then responding. It is time spent in the Word and in prayer. Jesus said in John

10:14, "I am the good shepherd; and I know My sheep, and am known by My own." And in verse 27, "My sheep hear My voice, and I know them, and they follow Me." The old adage "Practice makes perfect" is valid. The more time we spend with Jesus, the better able we are to recognize His voice, determine our purpose, and respond to Him.

SCRIPTURES ON YOUR PURPOSE

Proverbs 16:9—A man's heart deviseth his way: but the Lord directeth his steps.

Romans 8:28—And we know that all things work together for good to them that love God, to them who are the called according to his purpose.

John 15:16—Ye have not chosen me, but I have chosen you, and ordained you, that ye should go and bring forth fruit, and that your fruit should remain: that whatsoever ye shall ask of the Father in my name, he may give it you.

Matthew 28:19—Go ye therefore, and teach all nations, baptizing them in the name of the Father, and of the Son, and of the Holy Ghost:

Ecclesiastes 12:13—Let us hear the conclusion of the whole matter: Fear God, and keep his commandments: for this [is] the whole duty of man.

Isaiah 43:7—Even every one that is called by my name: for I have created him for my glory, I have formed him; yea, I have made him.

Isaiah 14:24—The Lord of hosts hath sworn, saying, Surely as I have thought, so shall it come to pass; and as I have purposed, so shall it stand:

Jeremiah 1:5—Before I formed thee in the belly I knew thee; and before thou camest forth out of the womb I sanctified thee, and I ordained thee a prophet unto the nations.

5

YES, MY SON

(GOD IS TALKING TO YOU; LISTEN)

Most churches in Indian Orchard, Massachusetts, were Roman Catholic. Many of my friends went to the big "white" church weekly to play Bingo or attend dances. One Saturday, curiosity drove me inside Saint Patrick's. In the chapel, an obviously drunk man was fast asleep on a pew.

Suddenly from the front of the sanctuary a man stepped into the aisle. I had no idea the man clad in black was called a priest. When he saw me, he said, "You are next; go behind that curtain. God wants to talk with you." He pointed to what looked like a very small room off to the side. I had no idea what I would find behind the drape, but I complied. I walked toward the booth, and once inside, a tiny door slid away. I could hear a disembodied voice ask, "Yes, my child?" It scared the living daylights out of me. I jumped up, fought my way through the curtain, and raced outside. I truly thought God was in that place with me.

Having survived my first encounter with the inside of a Catholic church, my curiosity got the better of me and I returned for a second visit. For some reason, on that day my need to go inside was stronger than any parental prohibition. I strode across the street, tugged on the heavy, wooden door, and slipped inside.

The first thing I noticed was the smell: a deep, dusky aroma. I would later learn it came from the incense and the candles. Then there was the architecture. Saint Patrick's ceiling rose up and up, and the sanctuary spread out around me. It was very different from the small, undecorated Pentecostal church where my dad and the others raised their hands and shouted "amen" on Sundays.

I could imagine that the Ruler of the universe would want to live in such a grand building with glittering candles and gilded statues of saints and angels rising behind the altar. With head bowed, I plopped down on the very first pew inside the front door and tried to pray. How long had I sat there? I don't know, but I did sense that someone had joined me. Jumping to my feet, heart racing, it was easy to believe I was in trouble for trespassing.

With great trepidation and reluctance, I looked up at the man who stood at the end of the pew. He was short, with graying hair, and wore a black suit with a white collar—much like the other man I had encountered on my first visit. His smile was gentle and his eyes kind. I explained that I just wanted to slip inside to pray. He welcomed me and then walked back down the aisle. I tried to figure out what I was supposed to do in this magnificent sanctuary: stand, sit, or kneel on the maroon velvet pad before me.

After several minutes I decide to kneel. About that time, the priest returned with something in his hand. He smiled, "Son, what's your name?"

"Michael," I answered quietly.

"That's a very good name—a biblical name, a kingly name. Do you have a Bible at home?"

"Only my father's; we all use it."

While sitting in the confessional at Immaculate Conception, I really thought the voice I heard was the voice of God speaking directly to me. The priest probably would have chuckled over my naïveté. Later in my life, I would learn that hearing Him speak directly to me was the greatest and most life-changing event I would ever experience. Hearing Him speak—through the Holy Spirit, through the still, small voice, through His Word—builds relationship and imparts purpose in our lives.

In Deuteronomy 28:1–2 (NKJV) we read:

> "Now it shall come to pass, if you diligently obey the voice of the Lord your God, to observe carefully all His commandments which I command you today, that the Lord your God will set you high above all nations of the earth. And all these blessings shall come upon you and overtake you, because you obey the voice of the Lord your God."

God intended that you and I hear His voice, follow His commandments, and then be overtaken by His blessings. This invaluable practice will reveal the purpose of God in our lives. Would your life be totally transformed by practicing His presence and attending to His voice? Every difficult situation—relationships, health, finances—could be changed by one single word from God. He knows the circumstances and He knows the Words that will effect change.

I'm reminded of the exchange between Eli and Samuel in 1 Samuel 3 (NKJV):

Now the boy Samuel ministered to the Lord before Eli. And the word of the Lord was rare in those days; there was no widespread revelation. And it came to pass at that time, while Eli was lying down in his place, and when his eyes had begun to grow so dim that he could not see, and before the lamp of God went out in the tabernacle of the Lord where the ark of God was, and while Samuel was lying down, that the Lord called Samuel. And he answered, "Here I am!" So he ran to Eli and said, "Here I am, for you called me."

And he said, "I did not call; lie down again." And he went and lay down.

Then the Lord called yet again, "Samuel!"

So Samuel arose and went to Eli, and said, "Here I am, for you called me." He answered, "I did not call, my son; lie down again." (Now Samuel did not yet know the Lord, nor was the word of the Lord yet revealed to him.)

And the Lord called Samuel again the third time. So he arose and went to Eli, and said, "Here I am, for you did call me."

Then Eli perceived that the Lord had called the boy. Therefore Eli said to Samuel, "Go, lie down; and it shall be, if He calls you, that you must say, 'Speak, Lord, for Your servant hears.'" So Samuel went and lay down in his place.

Now the Lord came and stood and called as at other times, "Samuel! Samuel!"

And Samuel answered, "Speak, for Your servant hears."

After Hannah, Samuel's mother, weaned the child, she fulfilled her promise: "I will give him to the LORD all the days of his life. . . " Samuel was taken to the temple in Jerusalem and placed in the care of Eli, a high priest. His life consisted of Torah instruction, working in the temple proper, and being overseen by godly men.

When Samuel grew older, his lessons and training became more intense. He was accustomed to hearing the voices of Eli and the priests calling him for an assignment during the daylight hours. Samuel's life changed dramatically, however, when he heard a voice during the midnight hour.

An obedient child, Samuel jumped from his bed, perhaps near the entrance to the holy of holies, and raced to the side of his mentor. Had Eli called him? No! After the third summons, Eli realized that Someone very special was beckoning his charge. Samuel was about to receive the first divine assignment of his life.

The ability to recognize the voice of God helps you and me to find the will of God. Jesus said in Matthew 4:4 (NKJV), "It is written, 'Man shall not live by bread alone, but by every word that proceeds [to go onward or forward; continue] from the mouth of God.'"

God doesn't speak to us just one time, but He continues to speak, and we will hear Him if we can but learn to listen.

Often, He speaks only a word or a phrase; He speaks hope, strength, correction, conviction or patience. The late Dr. Robert Schuller in a long-ago sermon said that God answers prayer in four ways: 1) When we are not ready, He says grow.; when the time is not right, He says slow; when we are not right, God says no; and when everything is right, He says go. When we listen to His voice, we learn to distinguish which answer is for the moment.

Too often during a church service we miss the one word God has for us because we are too focused on what someone is wearing, a new haircut, dress, or accessory, or the pastor's delivery. We must begin to concentrate intently on the *rhema*, the personal life-altering Word of the living God. To whom are you listening?

Paul wrote to Timothy of the importance of the Word in his second epistle, chapter 3, verses 16–17 (NKJV):

> All Scripture is given by inspiration of God, and is profitable for doctrine, for reproof, for correction, for instruction in righteousness, that the man of God may be complete, thoroughly equipped for every good work.

Jesus said in John 10:2–4 (NKJV):

> But he who enters by the door is the shepherd of the sheep. To him the doorkeeper opens, and the sheep hear his voice; and he calls his own sheep by name and leads them out. And when he brings out his own sheep, he goes before them; and the sheep follow him, for they know his voice.

In this world, the voices of men and of Satan clamor for attention in an attempt to be heard, rising above that still, small voice of the Holy Spirit. Listening for and to the voice of God prepares us for hearing and heeding. Is the voice heard the one trying to draw you and me into sin? If so, we can be assured it is not the voice of our Lord.

The Good Shepherd has never said that as His sheep, *perhaps* you and I will hear His voice, or we *might* hear His voice, or we *ought* to hear His voice. No; He said we *do* hear the voice of God. The problem is that all too often we don't recognize His voice. David urged in Psalm 46:10, "Be still, and know that I am God."

Elijah learned this lesson in 1 Kings 18. One anonymous writer provided his thoughts:

> Told that Jezebel, the wife of Ahab, king of Israel, was seeking [to] kill him, Elijah ran into the wilderness and collapsed in exhaustion. God sent an angel with food and water to strengthen him, told him to rest, and then sent him to Horeb. In a cave there, Elijah voices his complaint that all of God's prophets had been killed by Jezebel and he alone had survived. God instructed him to stand on the mountain in His presence. Then the Lord sent a mighty wind which broke the rocks in pieces; then He sent an earthquake and a fire, but His voice was in none of them.

After all that, the Lord spoke to Elijah in the still small voice, or "gentle whisper."

The point of God speaking in the still small voice was to show Elijah that the work of God need not always be accompanied by dramatic revelation or manifestations. Divine silence does not necessarily mean divine inactivity. Zechariah 4:6 tells us that God's work is "not by might nor by power, but by My Spirit," meaning that overt displays of power are not necessary for God to work.[10]

During a trip to Central America, and while in the company of a group of men that included Dr. Jose Coto, a noted El Salvadoran surgeon, we left the hotel for the vice president's residence to minister to his wife, who was ill. As we were driven through the streets, I noticed a dirty beggar whose arms and legs were terribly twisted.

As we passed by him, the Holy Spirit whispered that I was to stop and pray for him; I ignored that still, small voice and went on my way. When our entourage reached the vice president's palace, I literally could not get out of the car. The Holy Spirit again whispered that I would not have His blessing to pray for the wife unless I obeyed His earlier directive. I turned to the driver and asked him to take me back to the square. The car halted before the crippled man and we got out. Dr. Coto and I walked up to him and, as had the apostle Peter, I said: "Silver and gold I do not have, but what I do have I give you: In the name of Jesus Christ of Nazareth, rise up and walk" (Acts 3:6 NKJV).

Instantly, the man's limbs were straightened and strengthened and he began to praise God as he jumped up and ran down the street. People in cars and along the sidewalk stopped as the man gave his amazing testimony of God's power to heal. We then returned to the vice president's home, where Dr. Coto and I anointed the second lady of El Salvador and prayed for her.

Had I not heard and heeded the voice of God, our entourage would not have had the anointing of God that produced favor in the nation of El Salvador.

The most important aspect of hearing from God is that we just remain silent and listen. Lutheran pastor and theologian Dietrich Bonhoeffer was convinced that to effectively hear God's Word, we must practice His presence in silent contemplation:

We are silent at the beginning of the day because God should have the first word, and we are silent before going to sleep because the last word also belongs to God... Silence is nothing else but waiting for God's Word and coming from God's Word with a blessing. But everybody knows that this is something that needs to be practiced and learned, in these days when talkativeness prevails.[11]

SCRIPTURES ON LISTENING TO GOD

John 8:47—He that is of God heareth God's words: ye therefore hear them not, because ye are not of God.

John 10:27–28—My sheep hear my voice, and I know them, and they follow me:

Mark 4:24—And he said unto them, Take heed what ye hear: with what measure ye mete, it shall be measured to you: and unto you that hear shall more be given.

Psalm 37:4–5—Delight thyself also in the Lord; and he shall give thee the desires of thine heart.

Revelation 3:20—Behold, I stand at the door, and knock: if any man hear my voice, and open the door, I will come in to him, and will sup with him, and he with me.

Romans 10:17—So then faith cometh by hearing, and hearing by the word of God.

Job 33:14–15—For God speaketh once, yea twice, yet man perceiveth it not.

Proverbs 3:5–6—Trust in the Lord with all thine heart; and lean not unto thine own understanding.

John 10:2–4—But he that entereth in by the door is the shepherd of the sheep.

Psalm 37:7–9—Rest in the Lord, and wait patiently for him: fret not thyself because of him who prospereth in his way, because of the man who bringeth wicked devices to pass.

Psalm 119:105—Thy word is a lamp unto my feet, and a light unto my path.

James 1:22—But be ye doers of the word, and not hearers only, deceiving your own selves.

6

"THIS IS THE MORON"

(YOU ARE NOT WHAT *PEOPLE* SAY YOU ARE)

Jim was my best friend. We were just two guys hanging together after school, riding our bikes, and talking about what we wanted to do "when we grow up." We were typical except for the fact that his father treated him with kindness; to my father, I was "Moron." Not exactly a term of endearment, was it?

One Saturday afternoon, on our way home from school, Jim stopped by my house for a drink of water. We walked in the door, and were greeted with, "Hey, Moron, why'd you bring that half-breed in my house?" (Jim was part American Indian.) I was too afraid to comment on his rudeness lest I feel more than the sting of his tongue. His friends who were there chuckled uncomfortably, and I was mortified.

Not only had Dad insulted my closest friend, he was sitting at the kitchen table playing poker with a group of his buddies. Dad was in his underwear, knocking back glasses of Jack Daniel's.

Dad's name of choice for me was "Moron." Not once had I heard "I love you" from those lips that so tenderly and lovingly sipped on a glass of amber whiskey. Jack Daniel's was his friend; I, on the other hand, was "Moron."

By the time I was sixteen I had endured as much from Dad as I cared to take. Getting away from our house on Pasco Road became my number one priority. During the summer and later into the fall, I began searching for opportunities to extricate myself from the dysfunction and insanity that had become the normal routine in our family.

That November, while in the school library, we watched and listened in shock as televised news reports from Dallas, Texas, told us that President Kennedy had been assassinated. The Kennedy family was from Massachusetts, and although we didn't know them personally—and lived a life far removed from theirs—they seemed like one of our own. For us, President Kennedy's death was as much a personal matter as political or historic.

In the days surrounding that event and in the weeks that followed, Americans everywhere felt a renewed sense of patriotism. I was no less affected than anyone else and in the aftermath of President Kennedy's death, I decided to join the army, both as an expression of devotion to our country and as a means by which I could leave home. I'd been considering military service as an option already and the president's death made the decision all the more palatable. With conflict heating up in Vietnam and American troops still subject to skirmishes in Korea, the opportunity seemed tailor-made for me. As strange as it may seem, a war somewhere—anywhere—was a welcome opportunity to escape the war at home.

Jim and I decided we would enlist together on the "buddy system." We wanted to join the Eighty-Second Airborne. I'm sure we never noticed the irony of that choice. The Eighty-Second was a parachute division—I was afraid of heights. I couldn't pass the physical. (Jim did and was granted his wish.)

When we both turned seventeen, Jim and I took the military enlistment oath and were shipped to boot camp. Our dog tag numbers were sequential. My number was RA112052; his was RA112051. On the morning I left home, Mom made two bologna sandwiches for me and stuffed them in a sack with a banana and a candy bar. We were only going as far as Fort Dix, New Jersey, but she was a mother and I was her son, so she made lunch for me. I thought of it as her way of blessing me. She knew that once I left, I was never coming back.

Before long, I would be Korea bound! Our dream of staying together was shattered when Jim was sent to Vietnam. I had exchanged my fear of dying at my father's hand before I reached the age of twenty for a stint in Uncle Sam's army. I didn't know what to expect, but I soon learned that a little advance work is always profitable. As Pete Seeger, a twentieth-century American musician, said, "Education is what you get when you read the fine print; experience is what you get when you don't." I failed to read the fine print and found myself in the midst of one of life's most jarring experiences—army life. But I am sure the only reason I joined up was to get away from my father.

A parent's bullying tactics—whether physical, mental, verbal, or emotional—has an impact on children. The late Dr. James Lehman with Empowering Parents wrote, "When a parent shows aggression toward her child by using words that hurt, such as dummy, idiot, loser and jerk, she is likely doing it because of her own inadequacies."[12] The downside comes not only from the scars that are left on body, soul, and spirit, but in later life when the child might well become a carbon copy of the abusive parent.

As I previously wrote, my father learned early at the hand of *his* father that disobedience, real or perceived, brought swift retribution. Will Evans, who had also learned from his father, was an abusive man who ultimately passed that curse along to his son, Robert, my father. Through the power of the Holy Spirit and the blood of Jesus Christ, that curse has been broken. I was determined not to be like my dad when I grew up. I wanted to be the best father I could be to my children. I knew about "generational curses," and what the Bible said in Exodus 34:7: "I lay the sins of the parents upon their children and grandchildren; the entire family is affected—even children in the third and fourth generations" (NLT).

My grandfather was abusive, my father was abusive, but I was so grateful that the curse had been broken in my life at the age of eleven. It would not pass to my son or to his sons.

It would be the total antithesis of God's character for Him to place a load of guilt on an unsuspecting child because of the sins of the father. It is a reality, however, that the effects of sin can be felt from one generation to the next. If a father is an alcoholic and abusive, as was mine, the children learn those traits and may well fall into overindulgence or abuse. Too often children, perhaps unwittingly, choose to follow in the footsteps of their parents. When children are caught up in the sins of the parents, generations *can* be affected.

The cure for sin is and has always been the same: repentance. When a man or woman turns from a sinful lifestyle to serve Jehovah God, the curse is broken; they are saved. In Exodus 20:6 (NLT), God promises that He lavishes "unfailing love for a thousand generations on those who love me and obey my commands."

Do not allow a bully to define you or your worth. You are not defined by your eye color, skin color, IQ, or beauty. Neither are you defined by whether you are tall or short, disabled or not, whether your address is that of a mansion or an underpass. The author of *The Message* wrote in 1 Corinthians 7:17:

> And don't be wishing you were someplace else or with someone else. Where you are right now is God's place for you. Live and obey and love and believe right there. **God, not your marital status, defines your life**. Don't think I'm being harder on you than on the others. I give this same counsel in all the churches. (Emphasis mine)

You are a child of God, defined only by His love and

grace. Even more importantly, He loves you so much that had you been the ONLY one on planet Earth who needed to be redeemed, He would have died for *you*!

Perhaps you, like me, had a difficult childhood. Maybe abuse was an everyday occurrence. Likely you have scars, inside and out. An old African-American spiritual advises: "There is a balm in Gilead to make the wounded whole [the power to soothe and heal the broken-hearted]."

Past experiences, while difficult, may prove to be the catalyst for you or me to minister to another individual. A woman who has suffered abuse at the hands of a father or spouse could benefit from your story of deliverance and restoration. Such abuse may bring repeated opportunities to surrender our lives and ourselves to God as instruments of His peace, and to share His grace and love with others. Perhaps you could minister to a man who has lost his wife and children through death or divorce. It is through Him that we find peace and the true meaning of love.

In 1989, I was a guest minister at St. Mark's Methodist Church in Atlanta, Georgia. At the close of my sermon, I invited people who desperately needed a special blessing from God to come forward. As they did, my heart was drawn like a magnet to a young couple and their little girl who appeared to be about seven years old. The child had the eyes of a tormented old woman. The bitter tears rolling down the faces of the mother and father could only be the result of shattered, hopeless, desperate hearts.

The parents' palpable pain spilled onto me as I listened to their tale of horror. The father spoke in hushed tones, giving few details, sparing his fragile daughter more suffering. He shuddered before continuing: "Our little girl was kidnapped, held captive and abused for over a year. We've had her back home now almost six months, but she's still in such a state of shock she cannot talk, and she won't let me or other men touch her."

As tears coursed down my face, I knelt so that I was level with her and began to relate the painful abuse I endured as a child. As I quietly talked, it seemed that looking into her eyes was akin to staring into the broken windows of a dark, abandoned house. As I continued to share, a tiny light of hope flickered, then flamed, illuminating her little face.

Suddenly her lips quivered and hot tears began to roll down her cheeks. "Thank you!" she hiccupped. "Thank you!" She held out her hand to me, and when I clasped it she dropped a dollar bill into mine. (I still have that bill today.) She then buried her face in her mother's shoulder and began to cry, "Mama, Mama!" No one had to tell us her journey of healing had begun.

Every time I recall that precious little face, a strange mixture of joy and pain washes over me—joy because God's healing power was at work in that little girl's life, and pain for the thousands of other children, teenagers, and adults who endure insults, assaults, and atrocities more terrible than your worst nightmare. Am I exaggerating? I wish I were.

When you and I allow God to define us, His grace to cover us, His peace to enfold us, life becomes joyful. We, His children, are not defined by past sufferings, shortcomings, or setbacks. According to Ephesians 2:10 (NLT):

> For we are God's masterpiece. He has created us anew in Christ Jesus, so we can do the good things he planned for us long ago.

The people in the Samaritan village that housed the woman at the well likely didn't consider her God's masterpiece. When our Lord paused at the well, it was with a specific purpose. When the woman approached, He could have ignored her; instead, He chose to connect with her. It was an unprecedented step for a Jew to engage in conversation with a Samaritan. It was a social taboo for a man to be seen talking openly with an unknown female. It could have been misconstrued as an open invitation to a woman with loose morals, which would have reflected badly on Jesus.

But there was even more fodder for the gossips: This woman was known as an adulteress in the community. Her trip to the well in the middle of the afternoon was an attempt to avoid interacting with other women in the village. We are not certain that she was a prostitute, but that would have mattered little given what we *do* know: She had been married five times and was at that moment living with someone outside marriage. The woman was an outcast.

Mark Hall of the Christian band Casting Crowns penned the lyrics to a song that could have been written about this woman. It is titled, "Does Anybody Hear Her." Hall wrote:

> Does anybody hear her? Can anybody see?
> If judgment looms under every steeple
> If lofty glances from lofty people
> Who can't see past her scarlet letter
> And we never even met her
> Never even met her
> Does anybody hear her? Can anybody see?[13]

Jesus saw the woman walking toward Him, and although she avoided contact as she approached the well, our Lord was overcome with such great compassion that He spoke to her. Has that ever happened to you? Have you ever felt compelled by the Holy Spirit to approach a stranger?

Jesus struck up a conversation and then offered her eternal life—living water. If she accepted, He told her, she would never thirst again. She was offered a never-ending source of supply—from Him who is the Living Water—and Jesus gave her favor with all those in the village who had rejected her:

> The woman then left her waterpot, went her way into the city, and said to the men, "Come, see a Man who told me all things that I ever did. Could this be the Christ?" Then they went out of the city and came to Him. (John 4:28–30 NKJV)

When this woman shared the message of the good news, they were not only willing to associate with her but followed her back to the source of her joy—the Man waiting at the well. She had found it impossible to spend time with Jesus and not be changed. She might have shunned Him; she could have turned away as bereft as she was when she first arrived at the well, but she did not. The woman chose to accept the message of love and grace that Jesus offered, and her life was changed.

When you and I bow at His feet, we are no longer defined by our past; we become new creations in Christ Jesus—treasured beyond measure. Once I met Him, I was no longer "Moron"; I was His child.

In his second epistle to the Corinthians, chapter 5, verse 17, Paul wrote, "Therefore, if anyone is in Christ, he is a new creation; old things have passed away; behold, all things have become new" (NKJV).

What a wonderful thought! You and I can begin anew; our sins are gone and, according to the writer of Hebrews, God has declared, "I WILL REMEMBER THEIR SINS NO MORE." Our past sins have been cast into the Sea of Forgetfulness, forevermore forgotten! When you are haunted by the past, remember it is the tactic of the Enemy to bring condemnation. At these times, we need to return to 2 Corinthians and read chapter 10, verse 4 (NKJV), for another reminder from Paul:

> For the weapons of our warfare are not carnal but mighty in God for pulling down strongholds, casting down arguments and

every high thing that exalts itself against the
knowledge of God, bringing every thought
into captivity to the obedience of Christ,

You and I are constantly at war against Satan. He attacks us by employing our own thoughts. Rejoice! God has provided you and me with the shield of faith with which we "will be able to extinguish all the flaming arrows of the evil one" (Ephesians 6:16 HCSB).

Does anyone need to remind you or me that we are not perfect? Of course not. God, in His omniscience, knows that we are going to stumble and/or fall on our way to heaven. He also wants us to know that He has made provision for us to be picked up, dusted off, and to continue the race. He is ready to forgive—*and* forget. What joy to know that His grace is sufficient!

SCRIPTURES ON WHO I AM IN CHRIST

2 Corinthians 5:17—Therefore if any man be in Christ, he is a new creature: old things are passed away; behold, all things are become new.

1 Peter 2:9—But ye are a chosen generation, a royal priesthood, an holy nation, a peculiar people; that ye should shew forth the praises of him who hath called you out of darkness into his marvellous light:

Ephesians 2:10—For we are his workmanship, created in Christ Jesus unto good works, which God hath before ordained that we should walk in them.

John 1:12—But as many as received him, to them gave he power to become the sons of God, even to them that believe on his name:

2 Corinthians 5:21—For he hath made him to be sin for us, who knew no sin; that we might be made the righteousness of God in him.

John 15:5—I am the vine, ye are the branches: He that abideth in me, and I in him, the same bringeth forth much fruit: for without me ye can do nothing.

1 Corinthians 6:19—What? know ye not that your body is the temple of the Holy Ghost which is in you, which ye have of God, and ye are not your own?

Galatians 3:26—For ye are all the children of God by faith in Christ Jesus.

7

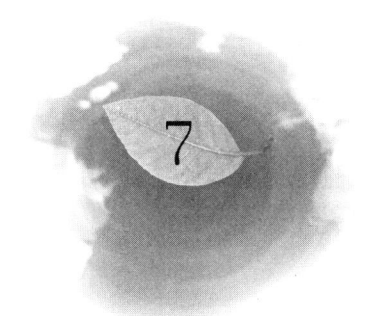

"I WILL BEAT YOU TO DEATH! GOD HATES LIARS."

(NO MATTER HOW GREATLY YOU HAVE BEEN LIED ABOUT, GOD IS FOR YOU)

Back then, it was every young boy's dream to have his very own knife. They were useful for so many things—whittling, carving initials into unsuspecting trees or fence posts, cleaning fingernails . . . all kinds of necessary activities. One day on the way home from school, I found a knife in the snow. I was excited because it was brand-new and still shiny. Eureka! My dream had come true! I snatched it up off the ground, stuck it in my pocket, and swaggered home. I couldn't wait to show Dad what some careless owner had dropped.

At dinner that night, I pulled my prized treasure from my pocket. With a big smile, I laid it on the table by Dad's plate, all the while hoping for a word of affirmation. Wrong move! He snatched it from my hand and snarled, "Where'd you steal that, Moron?"

My heart dropped quickly, as did my eyes. "I didn't steal it," I stuttered.

Dad stood so fast his chair toppled over. The clatter only served to enflame his anger. His voice took on a steely edge. "Don't lie to me. God hates liars and so do I!"

His face twisted with rage and he clenched his huge hands into fists. "For the last time, where did you get that knife? Tell me the truth now, or I will beat the @#$% out of you, Moron!"

"I found it in the snow," I cried.

"You're lying to me, Moron! Look me in the eye! You stole that knife, and I'm going to teach you what happens to liars!"

I was so completely panic-stricken I could not have made up a lie. I jumped up from my chair, never taking my eyes off him, and screamed, "I didn't steal it! I found it on the sidewalk in the snow. Someone must have dropped it just before I walked by." I edged around the back of the chair, considering my options.

"Moron, don't even think about running from me." His voice was deadly quiet. I would soon find out just how deadly.

I was backing toward the kitchen when Dad's hand snaked out and grabbed my arm with a viselike grip. Dad was about six feet four inches and weighed in at a good 250 pounds. In a single motion, he lifted me off the floor by one arm and carried me through the kitchen door and down the stairs into the basement. At the bottom of the old wooden stairs, he dropped me to the floor, grabbed an extension cord hanging on a nail and began swinging it in a circle, hitting me anywhere and everywhere. I jumped and twisted in an effort to avoid the cord, but he kept lashing—my head, neck, back, legs, arms.

I continued to protest my innocence; my father screamed, "You stupid moron! I'll beat you until you pee your pants, then I'll beat you for peeing!" My shirt ripped, and blood began to seep from the welts forming on my body. I screamed and begged him not to hit me until, spent, I could no longer cry out. As suddenly as rage had enveloped him, it ceased. He flung open the door to the canning cellar adjacent to the basement and heaved me inside. Slamming the door, he clicked the lock in place. I could hear him stalking up the stairs. When he reached the light switch, he turned off the light, leaving me alone in the dark canning cellar. I tried to open eyes, sticky with my own blood. When I finally pried them apart, I encountered only inky darkness.

I struggled to stand on lacerated, unsteady legs and, with arms outstretched, searched for the door. Ugh! I walked straight into a curtain of sticky cobwebs. They draped over my head and shoulders as I thrashed to brush them off. I didn't dare touch my face, wet with tears, for fear of what might be on my hands. Cobwebs! That meant spiders, and I was terrified of them.

Was that something crawling in my hair? With a whimper, I brushed frantically at my head, hoping to dislodge any creepy-crawlers that may have been in the web. It was then I felt the warmth and smelled the scent of urine as it trickled down my legs. I tentatively touched my pants, instinctively knowing they would be wet. I reached up to touch my burning shoulder and felt something warm and sticky seeping through the rips in my shirt. Blood!

New fears assailed me as I heard the scrabbling sounds of tiny feet. Rats! I froze in horror. I opened my eyes as wide as they would go but still could see nothing in the pitch-black cellar. I shivered; would I die here, my only companions the spiders and rats I so feared? My body throbbed with pain from the punches and kicks and lashes of the electric cord inflicted by the man who was supposed to love and protect me. Would the rats smell blood and attack? Were they waiting patiently in the dark for me to go to sleep so they could dine on the open wounds? All they probably needed was the smell of blood to stimulate their appetites.

In the quiet, I heard a sound on the other side of the cellar door. I froze: Had Dad returned to finish the job? Then came a whisper, "Mike, it's me, Jim. I'm going to unlock the door." Jim, my best friend, had been watching through the basement window as my dad beat me nearly lifeless. He watched until the kitchen door closed, then squeezed through the open window. He took the key off the nail by the door to the canning cellar and unlocked it. Helping me to the window, he shoved me through to the outside. With Jim supporting me, I stumbled across the yard and into the basement of Jim's house to escape my father. I didn't know what he would do when he opened the cellar door and found I was gone. I would have to deal with that later.

Dad must have regaled his friends with the story of the whipping he gave his lying son. The truth is that no matter how innocent you or I may be, lies hurt. Spanish philosopher Baltasar Grasian wrote, "A single lie destroys a whole reputation for integrity."[14] My father lied every time he called me "Moron," but for years I believed that lie. It was debilitating and arresting. In my childhood years, every time I heard that label, I bought into it—an adult said it was true; therefore, it must be.

First Corinthians 13:11 (NLT) gives us a glimpse into childhood:

> When I was a child, I spoke and thought and reasoned as a child. But when I grew up, I put away childish things.

As an adult, I realized that my father had many of the traits of a sociopathic personality:

- He was very charming and able to draw a crowd, whether it was at church or in the local nightclub.

- Conversely, he seemed to be unable to feel shame or remorse. He was an equal-opportunity victimizer.

- He thought himself above the law. His friends on the police force would not dare chastise him for his actions.

- He easily dominated young and old alike. He took his ire out on anyone who crossed him.

- He lived freely, seemingly without fear or guilt.

There came a time when I grasped that in order to move forward in the ministry to which God had called me, it was incumbent that I forgive my father for the abuse he heaped on his family. I heard the voice of God in my spirit asking, *"Will you let Me set you free of the destructive soul ties between you and your father? Will you go and seek his forgiveness?"*

I was stunned. "Whoa, Lord! Me ask his forgiveness? I was the one battered and beaten. I was the one physically, verbally, and emotionally abused. Shouldn't he be asking my forgiveness?"

Suddenly a scripture from Matthew 5:23–24 (NIV) flooded my soul:

> Therefore, if you are offering your gift at the altar and there remember that your brother or sister [or even your father] has something against you, leave your gift there in front of the altar. First go and be reconciled to them; then come and offer your gift.

I was offering God my life and whatever gifts and talents I possessed. I knew that my father would never come to me; it was up to me to go to him. I surrendered and said, "Yes, Lord, I will."

Despite the lies, abuse, lack of affection or affirmation, I went to my father and asked his forgiveness. Then wonder of wonders, I led him to Christ.

How does God want you and me to deal with liars and their lies, with those who make false accusations? Again, we turn to the Scriptures and the first lie ever recorded in Genesis 3:1–6 (NKJV):

> Now the serpent was more cunning than any beast of the field which the Lord God had made. And he said to the woman, "Has God indeed said, 'You shall not eat of every tree of the garden'?"
>
> And the woman said to the serpent, "We may eat the fruit of the trees of the garden; but of the fruit of the tree which is in the midst of the garden, God has said, 'You shall not eat it, nor shall you touch it, lest you die.'"
>
> Then the serpent said to the woman, "You will not surely die. For God knows that in the day you eat of it your eyes will be opened, and you will be like God, knowing good and evil."
>
> So when the woman saw that the tree *was* good for food, that it *was* pleasant to the eyes,

and a tree desirable to make one wise, she
took of its fruit and ate. She also gave to her
husband with her, and he ate.

The Bible does not reveal how long Adam and Eve had lived in the garden, nor if it was the first time "that old serpent" had visited them (see Revelation 12:9). Perhaps the two had seen the serpent lurking on the fringes or had even been tempted by him prior to this occasion. Eve, at least, seemed perfectly at ease in conversing with a snakelike beast.

The serpent slithered up to Eve and was cunning enough not to say, "Hey, Eve, God lied to you." The first tactic was to subtly plant the seed of doubt: "Has God not said?" She answered by patiently explaining to the questioner that they could safely eat of every tree in the garden except one. In Genesis 2:16b–17 (NKJV), God instructed Adam:

> Of every tree of the garden you may freely
> eat; but of the tree of the knowledge of good
> and evil you shall not eat, for in the day that
> you eat of it you shall surely die.

Notice, God didn't tell them not to *touch* the fruit, but rather not to *eat* of the fruit. Neither did He say they *might* die; God said they would *surely* die. Much has been written that God lied to the two garden dwellers, for they didn't fall down dead. When the two sinned and judgment was pronounced, the death penalty countdown began.

Satan realized quickly that Eve hadn't really comprehended what God had said regarding the Tree of Life. It was then that the Father of Lies lived up to his name: "God lied to you! You shall not surely die. You will just simply be as smart as He is." This is how Satan seeks to trick us; he simply convinces us that we misunderstood God's Word. The Creator wouldn't withhold anything from His dearly loved children. At some point you and I tend to become complacent; we want what we want when we want it. We are convinced that waiting or denial is not in God's plan. We lay down the shield of faith and become easy targets for Satan's fiery darts. The result: like Adam and Eve, we falter in our walk with God.

As soon as the first couple ate of the forbidden fruit, they realized the significance of their choice to defy God and immediately recognized that they were naked. In an attempt to hide their sin, the two covered themselves with fig leaves. (Couldn't they find anything else?) It was their way of handling their nakedness—the do-it-yourself way. However, God had a different plan. He killed an innocent animal—Genesis doesn't say what the animal was—and with the skin made "coats of skins" and clothed them. The lives of innocent animals were taken in order to cover the sin of Adam and Eve. It is a perfect picture of the obedience of Christ, who would give His life to cover the sins of the world and make it possible for man to stand righteous before God, the Father.

Jesus said, "I am *the* way" (see John 14:6). Not *a* way, THE way, and the only way. He said, "I am *the* truth." In Him and Him alone do we have eternal life, for there is no other way to the Father except through Jesus Christ. It is through His blood and His forgiveness that we can enjoy eternal life.

The Bible teaches forgiveness—everyone needs to be forgiven, and you and I need to forgive those who have wronged us. Not one of us is perfect, but we have access to God's forgiveness and His grace.

Conservative British politian Lord Balfour said:

> The best thing to give your enemy is forgiveness; to an opponent, tolerance; to a friend, your heart; to your child, a good example; to a father, deference; to your mother, conduct that will make her proud of you; to yourself, respect; to all men, charity.[15]

Luke 6:27–28 (NKJV) gives us definitive instructions in how to respond when verbally attacked:

> "But I say to you who hear: Love your enemies, do good to those who hate you, bless those who curse you, and pray for those who spitefully use you."

In this passage of scripture that sometimes seems so difficult to grasp, God is not reciting another list of "Do's." Instead, He is teaching a lesson on attitude. Today, signs with cute sayings pop up everywhere—on cards, letters, logos, in front of business establishments, and churches. Some make us smile, others cause embarrassment, but one causes introspection: "We may not be able to change our circumstances, but we can change our attitude."

First, Jesus tells us to love our enemies. We read in Proverbs 6:12, 14 (NLT) a description of the enemy:

> What are worthless and wicked people like? They are constant liars, . . . Their perverted hearts plot evil, and they constantly stir up trouble.

And yet, God admonishes us to bless and pray. According to pastor and blogger Dr. Jeremy Myers, our enemies are not "ministers ordained by God to show us our sins. When something a pastor says makes you think he's been reading your mail, and eavesdropping on your thoughts, that is the Holy Spirit using the pastor's words to get through to you. The pastor is not your enemy. . . any more than the Holy Spirit is . . . "[16]

Then He tells us how to love. We are to "do good," "bless," and "pray." Fuller Theological Seminary graduate and pastor Dr. Ralph Wilson wrote:

> If you are looking for a nice, comfortable religion that doesn't call for too many demands on your life, makes you feel better when you're down, and will reserve luxury suites for you in heaven when you die, then you probably shouldn't try to be one of Jesus' disciples. He is demanding. He has the crazy notion that his followers should serve others rather than themselves. He expects them to show integrity when no one is looking. And he expects them to love. Not just people who only occasionally have a bad day. But enemies? Jesus expects you to love your enemies.

Don't follow him unless you're ready to experience some discomfort.[17]

Next, Christ tells us to "bless." What? If you are from the South, you may have heard the expression to "bless someone out." It means to tell someone off without hesitation and in no uncertain terms. This is not what Christ means in Luke 6. He used the word *bless* to mean "applaud, sing the praises of, extol, speak well of, or rave about." Jesus admonished His followers to do the unexpected and "turn the other cheek." He meant that we are not to match insult with insult or retaliation with retaliation. That is how people in the world respond to a smear campaign. We are to go out of our way to bless that individual by word and deed.

Finally, we are to pray for that individual. Begin today to earnestly pray for your enemies. Make an effort to ask God to heal them—spiritually, emotionally, and physically. Pray for God to show mercy and grace to them. Oswald Chambers, author of the classic *My Utmost for His Highest*, wrote:

> God has established things so that prayer, on the basis of redemption, changes the way a person looks at things. Prayer is not a matter of changing things externally, but one of working miracles in a person's inner nature.[18]

Prayer not only changes *things*, it changes the one praying. The One to whom I pray is my Savior, my Lord, my Redeemer. It is He who, through His Word, teaches me to pray. As author C. S. Lewis wrote of prayer, "It doesn't change God—it changes me."[19]

SCRIPTURES ON GOD'S LOVE FOR US

John 3:16—For God so loved the world, that he gave his only begotten Son, that whosoever believeth in him should not perish, but have everlasting life.

Romans 5:8—But God commendeth his love toward us, in that, while we were yet sinners, Christ died for us.

1 John 4:19—We love him, because he first loved us.

Isaiah 41:13—For I the Lord thy God will hold thy right hand, saying unto thee, Fear not; I will help thee.

1 John 4:10—Herein is love, not that we loved God, but that he loved us, and sent his Son to be the propitiation for our sins.

Romans 8:35–39—Who shall separate us from the love of Christ? shall tribulation, or distress, or persecution, or famine, or nakedness, or peril, or sword?

Jeremiah 31:3—The Lord hath appeared of old unto me, saying, Yea, I have loved thee with an everlasting love: therefore with lovingkindness have I drawn thee.

1 John 4:8—He that loveth not knoweth not God; for God is love.

Galatians 2:20—I am crucified with Christ: nevertheless I live; yet not I, but Christ liveth in me: and the life which I now live in the flesh I live by the faith of the Son of God, who loved me, and gave himself for me.

8

"YOU WILL NEVER AMOUNT TO ANYTHING"

(GOD HAS HIDDEN GIFTS IN YOU;
HE HAS A PURPOSE FOR YOUR LIFE)

School was not a refuge for a boy who was regularly abused at home. There I was labeled "Kike." As a small child, I didn't understand that epithet. I thought they were saying "kite," and I knew I didn't own one. As if the abuse at home weren't enough, I was often bullied and beaten by the bigger kids for being a "Christ killer."

As early as junior high I began to skip school after my gym teacher at the junior high on Myrtle Street saw bruises on my back and legs. School officials visited my house twice. Blessedly, my father was away at work, and I found it necessary to lie about how I had received my injuries. Had I done anything else, I would have had to face my father's wrath when he came home. It became easier just to stay away from school while the bruises healed.

One incident that took place at school remains etched in my mind: I was so troubled at home that I could not focus in school. One day in English class, the teacher looked over a paper I had turned in and commented on my handwriting. (Because I have a chronic neurological movement disorder, a form of dystonia, it is almost impossible for me to hold a pen or pencil and write legibly. At the time, I was not aware of that problem.) She declared with some condescension, "Michael, you will never be a writer. This effort is unacceptable," and then slashed a big red zero across the center of the page.

Neither my teacher nor I had an inkling of what God could and would do in my life. One day, as an adult, a particularly hurtful episode in my life played out—being betrayed by a man to whom I had loaned my life savings. Shortly after I discovered his duplicity, I wrote the word *Return* on a scrap of paper. As I held it up before God, I felt impressed to write a book and call it *The Return*. Within ninety days, the book was a reality and in the next twelve months had become a blockbuster bestseller. The royalties from sales were exactly seven times what had been stolen from me.

One of the most liberating truths you and I can discover is that Christ has a definite purpose for our lives; and He will bestow on us the gifts necessary to achieve His plan.

We have the choice of whether or not to connect with what God has already provided. It is just as if I went to the store and bought a present for my wife, then took it home and gave it to her. Though it was bought and paid for and truly belongs to her, she will never be able to use it until she decides to unwrap the box and accept the gift.

So it is with God's will for our lives. Jesus paid the price for our total salvation through His death on the cross. Unless you and I are willing to receive His gift, it is forever lost to us. No matter how much our hearts cry out to have His will and purpose accomplished in our lives, we must first receive His gift of salvation according to His Word.

The purpose for my life—and for the life of every Christian on this earth—is to stand in agreement with our Lord and Savior, just as I stood in agreement with His will for me to be saved. It was as if a giant vacuum had begun to remove the dross from my life—the clouds of confusion vanished from my mind, and the burdensome *oughts* and *shoulds* fell off my shoulders. The answer to every person's identity, destiny, inferiority, or insecurity can be found in Christ.

Sadly, you and I often find ourselves with no sense of purpose, or we feel we are bereft of the gifts needed to achieve God's will on earth. We have no sense of destiny, little sense of purpose, and are indistinguishable from those who seek little else but their own selfish desires. A story is told of Dr. Albert Schweitzer, the renowned German theologian and physician:

> "Be doers of the word, and not hearers only, deceiving yourselves" [James 1:22]. In 1953 reporters gathered at a Chicago railway station waiting to meet the 1952 Nobel Peace Prize winner. He was a big man, six-feet-four tall with bushy hair and a large mustache. Reporters were excited to see him and expressed what an honor it was [to] meet him. Cameras were flashing, compliments were being expressed—but seeing beyond the adulation the visitor noticed an elderly Afro-American woman struggling to carry her two large suitcases.
>
> "Excuse me," he said as he went to the aid of this woman. Picking up her cases, he escorted her to a bus and then apologized to the reporters for keeping them waiting.

The man was Dr. Albert Schweitzer, the famous missionary-doctor who had invested his life helping poor and sick people in Africa. A member of the reception committee remarked to one of the reporters, "That's the first time I ever saw a sermon walking."[20]

God gave Dr. Schweitzer the gift of compassion and helps. He sensed the need of the lady in the crowd; but not stopping there, he stepped out to offer practical help. There are those who spend an entire lifetime trying to figure out their purpose in the Christian life. They constantly question: What does God want me to do? I can confirm to you that spending time searching for a lofty assignment is *not* what God expects of me and you.

First, we need to commit our lives to doing what we *know* to do. Just be yourself; do not try to emulate another. The Bible has given us some very specific things that we, as Christians, are to do—nothing flashy, simply practical. The initial assignment God has given His followers is to reach the lost with the message of salvation. Next, we are to encourage people to follow Christ. Third, and sometimes the most difficult, we are to love each other. Paul reminds us in Colossians 3 that we are to be tender, merciful, kind, patient, forgiving, loving, and joyful.

As children of God, you and I should look for opportunities to lighten someone's burden—to reach out in love to the lost, the sick, and those hurting emotionally. Each gift God has given you and me is unique. We are not all called to be a Billy Graham, a Billy Sunday, or even a Bill Hybels (of Willow Creek Community Church fame). Many of us cannot sing like Sandi Patty or the late George Beverly Shea, Yolanda Adams or Michael English, Amy Grant or BeBe Winans; yet David tells us in Psalm 100 that we are to "make a joyful noise unto the Lord."

First and foremost, God wants the gift of *you*—your time, your knowledge, your gifts, your expertise. The most generous contributors have given their lives for the cause of the gospel; others serve on mission fields at home and abroad. Many have given their time and talents to the Lord—preaching, singing, encouraging, and ministering to the homeless, spending time daily in prayer and intercession.

In this modern-day "me-first" society, instead of doing it God's way, we've done it *our* way. James 1:17 (NKJV) says, "Every good gift and every perfect gift is from above, and comes down from the Father of lights . . . " We need to acknowledge God's provision and offer the praise due Him. He is the Source of every good thing—life, health, opportunity, talent, and blessing. God is Jehovah-Jireh—our Provider.

God's purpose for your life and mine will always be in perfect alignment with His Word. Scottish theologian William Barclay said: "There are two great days in a person's life—the day we are born and the day we discover why."[21] One of Satan's greatest ploys is to make us believe that living the Christ-life is always just out of our reach. He would have us idolize certain men and women of God just as a teenager might idolize a rock star or sports hero. The devil would have us think, *Oh, if only I could be like them! But it must take such great talent and determination to do what they do. It is so far beyond anything I could ever do!*

There is the deception: *If only I could be like them.* Well, guess what? You *are* like them! If you are a Christian, then you have inside you the same Holy Spirit others have. You too have Jesus as Lord and Savior, and you have a heavenly Father who loves you and wants to know and be known by you. In God's eyes, all that matters is your obedience to His will. Large meetings don't matter. Big churches don't matter. Incredible mission outreaches don't matter. If they are of God, then they are merely by-products of Believers who have obeyed Him. *The important thing is the obedience.*

One small verse hidden in Luke 2:52 is an open window on the early life of Christ. It reads, "And Jesus increased in wisdom and stature, and in favor with God and men" (NKJV). Jesus also grew in stature: He became grounded in education, physical health, moral teachings, and social interaction. Rather than proclaim to Joseph and Mary the importance of His mission, Jesus humbled himself and went home to Nazareth, where He worked alongside Joseph in the carpenter shop, sat beside him in the synagogue, and learned obedience. His entire life was one of obedience, to His earthly parents and to His heavenly Father.

Jehovah God's blessings cannot be separated from obedience to His Word. This is never more obvious than in Deuteronomy 28: 1, 2, 15 (KJV):

> If thou shalt hearken diligently unto the voice of the Lord thy God, to observe and to do all his commandments . . . all these blessings shall come on thee, and overtake thee, . . . But it shall come to pass, if thou wilt not hearken unto the voice of the Lord thy God, to observe to do all his commandments . . .

that all these curses shall come upon thee, and overtake thee."

Moses delivered this bountiful promise of Yahweh's blessings on His children if they would but obey God's commands. If they rebelled, He likewise swore the people would be cursed—cruelly cursed. Moses declared that life and blessing was in obedience to God's Word; death and destruction resided in disobedience.

How, then, can you discover the blessings of God for your life? As Moses warned the children of Israel in Deuteronomy 28:1 (NIV), obedience is the key that unlocks the door to Yahweh's abundant blessings:

> If you fully obey the Lord your God and carefully follow all his commands I give you today, the Lord your God will set you high above all the nations on earth.

A loving, active, vibrant relationship with God is vital. As you live and walk daily with Him, blessings and benefits follow. Obedience and faith go hand in hand. One cannot exist without the other. Strong faith touches the heart of God and moves the hand of God. Obedience opens the door and releases the blessings of God, as Deuteronomy 28:2 (NKJV) records: "These blessings shall come upon you and overtake you." Can you imagine not being able to outrun God's abundance in your life? Being blessed simply means having the supernatural power of God at work in your life.

That great orator and preacher Charles Spurgeon said of obedience:

> Having once discerned the voice of God, obey without question. If you have to stand alone and nobody will befriend you, stand alone and God will befriend you.[22]

The psalmist wrote:

> Except the Lord build the house, they labor in vain that build it: except the Lord keep the city, the watchman waketh but in vain.
>
> It is vain for you to rise up early, to sit up late, to eat the bread of sorrows: for so he giveth his beloved sleep. (Psalm 127:1–2 KJV)

We can work hard, stay up late, and arise early, but none of it matters if we are building a kingdom unto ourselves rather than unto God. In fact, the opposite is true: If we are obeying God, we won't be working impossibly long hours to build His kingdom, because He gives his beloved sleep and rest. The only real work is staying in our quiet place until we learn His purpose for our lives. Then we simply have to live it out. The rest will take care of itself.

About one hundred years before Samuel lived, there was a judge named Gideon. When he was called, the Israelites were in subjugation to the Midianites, a warrior tribe descended from Abraham through one of his wives, Keturah (Genesis 25:1–2 KJV). Under the thumb of the Midianites, the Israelites lived not in houses in the promised land but in caves and crevices in the rocks. Plenty had been replaced with paucity, with hunger and lack.

Each year during the harvest, the Midianites would descend like locusts upon the country and destroy the fields. After seven long years of being preyed upon, the Israelites began to pray for deliverance. One day, as Gideon was threshing wheat in a secluded spot, an angel of the Lord suddenly stood before him:

> And the Angel of the Lord... said to him, "The Lord is with you, you mighty man of valor!" Gideon said to Him, "O my lord, if the Lord is with us, why then has all this happened to us? And where are all His miracles which our fathers told us about, saying,

'Did not the Lord bring us up from Egypt?' But now the Lord has forsaken us and delivered us into the hands of the Midianites." (Judges 6:12–13 NKJV)

Gideon had yet to learn it is we who turn our backs on Him, the Giver of life and peace, Jehovah-Shalom. He was about to discover that God does not forsake His own, that Radical Obedience brings the Favor of God.

Gideon had been chosen by God to engage the entire Midianite army in battle. Gideon's first reaction to God's instructions was one of disbelief. He was no valiant warrior; he was in hiding from the enemy while threshing wheat. Not a very courageous beginning for a deliverer. Gideon was from the tribe of Manasseh, from its most inconsequential family. He was the youngest son, and in his own words, "the least in my father's house" (see Judges 6:15 NKJV). He could not comprehend that God wanted *him* for the task at hand. He was not some superhero—he was a simple man with little to commend him as a soldier. He had two things in his favor—willingness and obedience. Hudson Taylor, the great pioneer missionary to China, might well have described Gideon's life when he said, "I have found that there are three stages in every great work of God: first, it is impossible, then it is difficult, then it is done."[23]

To confirm the call on his life, Gideon asked for a sign. God acquiesced to his request and gave him not one but several signs. After God had repeatedly confirmed the call on Gideon's life, Gideon issued the call for the people to gather. He was amazed when 32,000 assembled. He looked around at the number of people and must have been stunned by the size of the crowd.

But God had other plans! He told Gideon that the group was too large and needed to be pared down. Why? God didn't want the people to think they had won the battle on their own merit; He wanted it known far and wide that the God of Abraham, Isaac, and Jacob fought for His people. Gideon was advised to send home all who were fearful. That cut the ranks by two-thirds—down to only 10,000 men. Still, God deemed there were too many. He devised one further test:

> "Everyone who laps from the water with his tongue, as a dog laps, you shall set apart by himself; likewise everyone who gets down on his knees to drink." And the number of those who lapped, putting their hand to their mouth, was three hundred men; but all the

> rest of the people got down on their knees to drink water. Then the Lord said to Gideon, "By the three hundred men who lapped I will save you, and deliver the Midianites into your hand." (Judges 7:5–7 NKJV)

Three hundred men! That was Gideon's army. The Midianite army was said to be "without number" (see Judges 7:12). Yet Gideon obeyed God's specific instructions. Each man was to carry a trumpet and a pitcher with a torch inside. The men were divided into three companies of one hundred each and disbursed around the perimeter of the Midianite camp. At the appointed time, they were to blow the trumpets, smash the lamps and yell, "The sword of the Lord and of Gideon" (Judges 7:20b NKJV).

Total pandemonium seized the enemy camp. The mighty Midianite army fled before the army of the Lord. Gideon pursued the enemy until it was vanquished.

Gideon could have walked away from God's plan at any time. In the natural, it must have seemed totally impossible to win Israel's freedom from the marauding, murderous Midianites. However, Gideon chose to obey the call of God.

When you and I, like Gideon, surrender our own preconceived ideas of how to win the battle, it will bring victory, deliverance, and peace.

SCRIPTURES ON GOD'S GIFTS

James 1:17—Every good gift and every perfect gift is from above, and cometh down from the Father of lights, with whom is no variableness, neither shadow of turning.

Romans 6:23—For the wages of sin is death; but the gift of God is eternal life through Jesus Christ our Lord.

Ephesians 2:8—For by grace are ye saved through faith; and that not of yourselves: it is the gift of God:

John 3:16—For God so loved the world, that he gave his only begotten Son, that whosoever believeth in him should not perish, but have everlasting life.

Romans 12:6—Having then gifts differing according to the grace that is given to us, whether prophecy, let us prophesy according to the proportion of faith;

Galatians 2:20—I am crucified with Christ: nevertheless I live; yet not I, but Christ liveth in me: and the life which I now live in the flesh I live by the faith of the Son of God, who loved me, and gave himself for me.

Acts 2:38—Then Peter said unto them, Repent, and be baptized every one of you in the name of Jesus Christ for the remission of sins, and ye shall receive the gift of the Holy Ghost.

Matthew 6:1–34—Take heed that ye do not your alms before men, to be seen of them: otherwise ye have no reward of your Father which is in heaven.

Romans 8:38–39—For I am persuaded, that neither death, nor life, nor angels, nor principalities, nor powers, nor things present, nor things to come . . .

9

"WHEN I GROW UP . . . I WANT TO BE TWENTY"

(YOUR DAYS ARE IN HIS HANDS)

As an abused child with no self-esteem, school was a challenge. One encounter at school has been forever etched in my mind, and it had nothing to do with abuse. One Monday in my fifth-grade class at Indian Orchard Elementary School, our teacher informed us that the following day—Tuesday—he would ask each of us what we wanted to be when we grew up. I obsessed about the question all night. The following morning, I would have done just about anything not to have to go to school. I couldn't think of a plausible excuse that would not incur the wrath of my father.

That afternoon, as one child after another revealed his or her dream of being a teacher, doctor, lawyer, nurse, policeman, fireman, actress, or dancer, I tried to make myself as small as I could in hopes he would pass over me. I hunkered down in my seat on the last row near the door, just under the red bell, and refused to raise my hand as many had done. Not only did I not want to answer the question, I didn't want to face the added ridicule of stuttering my way through it.

I heard Mr. Maurice's voice grow louder and lifted my head enough to see that he had stopped beside my desk. I was perspiring profusely because I was wearing two pairs of pants and three undershirts. I thought it would make everyone think I was bigger.

I was so skinny that the kids laughed and made fun of me. I heard dozens of skinny jokes, such as, "You're so skinny I bet you have to jump around in the shower to get wet!"

"Michael Evans. Quit wool-gathering and answer my question. What do you want to be when you grow up?"

With eyes downcast, I hesitatingly answered, "Twenty."

The kids began to giggle.

"What? What did you say?" he demanded.

"I want to be twenty."

"No, you misunderstood me," he said. "Do you want to be a lawyer, a teacher, maybe a policeman?"

"No," I repeated. "I want to be twenty." The whole class burst into laughter.

When the dismissal bell rang, I ran out of the classroom trying to hide my tears. I had said exactly what I meant. I didn't believe I would live to be twenty years old. I thought surely my father would kill me before then. I didn't have any dream or vision other than to be twenty.

Although I was certain my days were numbered, like King David, I would eventually learn Who it is that numbers my days. He wrote in Psalm 31:15, "My times are in your hand" (ESV).

I could declare with complete confidence, as did the writer of Hebrews:

> Therefore, we may boldly say: The Lord is my helper; I will not be afraid. What can man do to me? (Hebrews 13:6 HCSB)

My friend, how long will you live on planet Earth? Will you wake up in the morning? Will your heart continue to beat after you fall asleep tonight? How long before your loved ones gather around your bed and bid you farewell? The answer to all those questions: Only God knows.

Rev. Andrew Murray, a South African writer, teacher, and pastor wrote a letter to encourage a lady facing great distress. In time of trouble say:

> First, [God] brought me here, it is by His will I am in this straight place: in that fact I will rest. Next, He will keep me here in His love, and give me grace to behave as His child. Then, He will make the trial a blessing, teaching me lessons He intends for me to learn, and working in me the grace He means to bestow. Last, in His good time He can bring me out again—how and when He knows. Let me say I am here, (1) By God's appointment, (2) In His keeping, (3) Under His training, (4) For His time.[24]

"In His good time." How easy to say; how hard to live out.

It was easy for me to believe that I would die by my father's hand any day; not quite so easy to believe that God could deliver me.

The story of Richard Wurmbrand is riveting. He was a minister of the gospel who had been imprisoned for his stand against communism. He suffered through years of incarceration and the most brutal of tortures before $7,000 was paid for his ransom. He and his family emigrated from Romania to the United States, where Richard and his wife, Sabina, devoted the remainder of their lives to aiding Christians persecuted for their beliefs.

Before his death in 2001, I was honored to share a meal with Wurmbrand. As we talked that evening, I posed some questions about his experiences in the communist prison camps. "Did you ever feel as if you were losing your mind?" I asked. He said that he had but gave those feelings to Christ so he did not have to worry. He also said that when he suffered heartache for his family, he gave those emotions to Christ as well. Finally, he gave his body to Christ and no longer needed to worry about his health. Armed with complete death to his flesh, the communist prison guards and interrogators no longer had the power to hurt him.

"The guard came for me one day and threatened, 'You must realize that I can break your arms, your legs, anything I want,'" Wurmbrand told me. "I answered him, 'If you break my arm, I will say, *God loves you* and if you break my leg I will say, *I love you too.*'" He said the stoic guard began to cry at his answer, and Wurmbrand was able to lead him to Christ that day.

Patience in tribulation, the love of Christ, and the joy of the Lord that passes understanding enabled Wurmbrand to gain favor with a prison guard who was, perhaps unknowingly, searching for truth. That is a trait sadly missing in this modern-day "get it now" generation.

Patience is one virtue that genuinely requires trust in God's divine sovereignty. There are days when the valley is as dark as the bottom of a cavern; God seems to have abandoned us with no way to light the path. Our prayers seem to go no farther than a brass ceiling—totally impenetrable. At those times, we are prone to feel that we have been forsaken. I've had days like that, haven't you? It is at that moment we must pose the question: "Has God really forsaken me?" Why would He do that now? He promised in His Word that He would never leave us or forsake us. In Romans 3:4 (NLT) we read: "Even if everyone else is a liar, God is true." Again in Numbers 23:19 (HCSB), Moses reveals a basic truth about God:

> God is not a man who lies, or a son of man who changes His mind. Does He speak and not act, or promise and not fulfill?

Why does it sometimes seem that our patience is stretched to its limit? It could be that God is working to develop that characteristic in us. It is not a passive process; it is active. We want to move forward; we want to reach our objective. We don't want to wait until God says, "Go." The obstacles He places in our lives are designed to build our endurance, to prepare us for the troubles that are certain to come. Look at the opportunities that often come our way in the midst of tribulation. In the middle of Pharaoh's murderous rage, Jacobed, Moses' mother, saved her son who would deliver the Israelites.

God desires to do something in your life to form His character in you. He wants you to look and act like Jesus! Sometimes He allows pressure to build as a way of refining your patience and faith. You are more important to God than the issues you face. The stress and pressures are temporary. Remember that. They will pass in time. You must be strong enough to face them as a man or woman of faith.

Jesus died so you could have abundant life. He did not die for issues or causes. He died for *you*. He also rose again, making you a conqueror in Him. You will overcome the pressures of life when you recognize His love and care for you, and submit to His lordship.

As Christians, we are not exempt from the pressure of tribulation. Some face it head on; others duck and run. The great temptation is not to "run with endurance the race that is set before us" (Hebrews 12:1 NKJV) but to run to the pill bottle, alcohol, or the needle. We may even blame God rather than the one whose sole job is to "steal and kill and destroy" (John 10:10 NIV). There are those who actually realize that God is at work, attempting to make them stronger, to build faith, endurance, and perseverance.

In John 8:44 (NKJV), Jesus identified the problem with the consummate liar, "When he [Satan] speaks a lie, he speaks from his own resources, for he is a liar and the father of it." The Father of Lies constantly tries to tell you and me that God has abandoned us. I'm reminded of the prophet Elijah, who challenged the 400 prophets of Baal in 1 Kings 18:25–27 (NKJV):

> "Choose one bull for yourselves and prepare it first, for you are many; and call on the name of your god, but put no fire under it." So they took the bull which was given them, and they prepared it, and called on the name of Baal from morning even till noon, saying, "O Baal, hear us!" But there was no voice; no one answered. Then they leaped about the altar which they had made. And so it was, at noon, that Elijah mocked them and said, "Cry

aloud, for he is a god; either he is meditating, or he is busy, or he is on a journey, or perhaps he is sleeping and must be awakened."

Satan wants us to believe that Almighty God is meditating, or busy, or on vacation, or taking a nap, or even dead. The truth is that God is love, and He loves you and me—unconditionally. Deuteronomy 33:27 reminds us, "The eternal God is your refuge, and underneath are the everlasting arms; He will thrust out the enemy from before you . . . " (NKJV). Put the Enemy on notice: You are a child of God and He holds you in His arms, just as a loving father holds a frightened child and offers comfort.

In May 1891, author and pastor Rev. C. H. Spurgeon preached a sermon at Metropolitan Tabernacle, Newington, England. He expounded on David's psalm and said:

> We assent to the statement, "My times are in thy hand," as to their result. Whatever is to come out of our life, is in our heavenly Father's hand. He guards the vine of life, and he also protects the clusters which shall be produced thereby. If life be as a field, the field is under the hand of the great Husbandman, and the harvest of that field is with him

also. The ultimate results of his work of grace upon us, and of his education of us in this life, are in the highest hand. We are not in our own hands, nor in the hands of earthly teachers; but we are under the skillful operation of hands which make nothing in vain. The close of life is not decided by the sharp knife of the fates; but by the hand of love. We shall not die before our time, neither shall we be forgotten and left upon the stage too long.[25]

As a child, I was certain I would not live to see my twentieth birthday. Contrarily, God has blessed me with an additional fifty-plus years and a work that He has consecrated unto Himself. Through no effort of my own, I have met kings, princes, prime ministers, presidents, and diplomats. God made it possible to purchase the Corrie ten Boom House in Haarlem, Holland, and build the Friends of Zion Heritage Center and Museum in Jerusalem. I have been blessed with a wonderful, godly wife, four children, and ten grandchildren so far. It has been an amazing journey and I look forward to what He has in store during whatever the next phase of my life proves to be.

SCRIPTURES ON GOD'S PROTECTION

Psalm 91:1–4—He who dwells in the secret place of the Most High shall abide under the shadow of the Almighty. I will say of the Lord, "He is my refuge and my fortress; my God, in Him I will trust." Surely He shall deliver you from the snare of the fowler and from the perilous pestilence. He shall cover you with His feathers, and under His wings you shall take refuge; His truth shall be your shield and buckler.

Psalm 91:7–8—A thousand may fall at your side, and ten thousand at your right hand; but it shall not come near you. Only with your eyes shall you look, and see the reward of the wicked.

Psalm 46:1–2—God is our refuge and strength, a very present help in trouble.

Psalm 32:7—You are my hiding place; You shall preserve me from trouble; You shall surround me with songs of deliverance.

Psalm 5:11—But let all those rejoice who put their trust in You; let them ever shout for joy, because You defend them; let those also who love Your name be joyful in You.

Psalm 34:8—Oh, taste and see that the Lord is good; blessed is the man who trusts in Him!

Psalm 61:4—I will abide in Your tabernacle forever; I will trust in the shelter of Your wings.

Psalm 118:8—It is better to trust in the Lord than to put confidence in man.

John 10:29—My Father, who has given them to Me, is greater than all; and no one is able to snatch them out of My Father's hand.

Isaiah 41:10 Fear not, for I am with you; be not dismayed, for I am your God. I will strengthen you, yes, I will help you, I will uphold you with My righteous right hand.

10

"STOP IT!!"

(YOUR GREATEST PAIN IS THE KEY TO YOUR POWER AND PURPOSE)

Friday night was date night for Dad. He would drench himself with Old Spice cologne and sing a chorus or two of "Ghost Riders in the Sky" or "Rawhide" while he slipped into his best shirt and pants. He was going to check out the "babes" who hung out at the neighborhood bar. He would make his way to the Twilight Café to get roaring drunk and then bed his girlfriends. By the time the bar closed and Dad staggered home, a few drinks had turned into full-blown drunkenness.

As soon as Dad was out the door, Mom would feed us kids and we would play in the street until bath time. Clean and clad in our pajamas, we sat in the living room and watched *Rin Tin Tin* and then *Walt Disney Presents*. I loved those shows. The good guys always won. The dog saved the day, and wishes really did come true. Maybe it was seeing those shows that sparked the wish that I would live to see my twentieth birthday.

Strangely, I was never angry with my father. I figured I deserved the beatings. I never considered that I was abused; I thought all dads were like that, and that my childhood was painful but normal.

Long before Dad was due to stagger back from the bar, we were hurried off to bed, but I couldn't sleep through his ranting and raving when he crossed the threshold after his evening out with the guys—or gals. His trips to the bar became, for all of us, nights of fear. I slept under my bed—not so far under that I couldn't see what little light seeped into the room and not quite far enough to risk a spider that might be hiding in a corner. Like the ostrich hiding its head in the sand, I thought Dad couldn't find me there. We dreaded to hear the front door open and slam shut in the wee hours of Saturday morning when he made his way home.

Dad would often shove Mom into a chair at the base of the stairs and take his frustrations out on her with his fists. One night, I awoke to the sounds of the usual beating and used my pillow to cover my head and drown out the terrified screams and sounds of flesh on flesh rushing up from below. About two-thirty in the morning, during a lull in the mayhem downstairs, I eased from under the bed and crept down the hallway to the top of the stairs. I sat there with my arms wrapped around me, tears cascading down my face, listening to my mom's whimpers as Dad continued to beat her.

Then he must have gotten a second wind, or perhaps another shot of Jack Daniel's, because the yelling began again. "You Jew whore!" he screamed. "Tell me about that bastard moron upstairs. You know he's not mine! I went off to the army and you whored around and spread your legs for any big-nosed Jew in town. Tell me the truth!"

With every sentence, he hit her with his open palm, but he was so strong and his hands so large that it must have been like being hit in the head with a frying pan. His insults were as ferocious as his punches. Suddenly it made sense even to my eleven-year-old mind. I knew why my mother wore sunglasses so often. It was my fault! He was beating my mother because of me. I must be a really bad person to make my dad hit my mom because of me. I knew what that word meant; I'd heard it at school. He thought I belonged to some other man. I hung my head in shame. I hated myself as much as my father hated me. I wished I had never been born.

Mother tried to protest her innocence, but the whiskey deadened Dad's senses. He was convinced he was right. He was always right, and there was no way to persuade him otherwise. Dad's motto must have been, "My mind is made up; don't confuse me with the facts."

The next blow brought her chair crashing to the floor. I eased far enough down the stairs to see that Mom, who had been sitting in the chair, now lay on the kitchen tile sobbing and curled up in a fetal position. As Dad lifted his hand to strike her again, I could take it no longer. I screamed, "Stop it!" Dad whipped around and, despite his size, flew up the stairs. I ran for dear life. He followed me into my room and lashed into me with his fists. (Years later I discovered that I had suffered hairline fractures in both arms that night.) He grabbed me just inside the door of my room and raised me as high as he could reach over his head. My feet were dangling several feet off the floor.

"Moron Jew!" he forced out between clenched teeth. "You're gonna regret the day you were born!" His meaty hands closed like a vise around my neck and he swung me back and forth as if I were a pendulum; his grip grew tighter and tighter. I kicked at him and tried to pry his fingers from my throat. The more I fought, the stronger his grip became. I looked into the face of my father, the man who was supposed to love me, and saw only deadly rage. I was sure no father could hate a son more than he hated me. I saw murder in his eyes and could not breathe. Consciousness began to ebb away; I was certain my life was about to end. He tossed me on the floor in a broken heap. I inched to the center of the room, barely aware of my surroundings, gasping for every breath. The pain was so intense I scarcely remember heaving up the contents of my stomach.

Sometime later I awoke, my body curled into a fetal position. My face and pajamas were covered in dried vomit. My body ached. I tried to push myself up from the floor of that dark room but fell back, the room spinning. I closed my eyes, clenching my fists in total agony. Shaking uncontrollably, I cried out the first prayer I had ever prayed: "Why was I born? Why?!"

There are many words to describe God: Creator, eternal, love, omnipotent, omnipresent, omniscient, holy, righteous, merciful. One of the words we seldom use is "compassionate." It means gentle, caring, empathetic. We see it used in Exodus 34:6 (NIV):

> And he passed in front of Moses, proclaiming, "The Lord, the Lord, the compassionate and gracious God, slow to anger, abounding in love and faithfulness . . ."

Our heavenly Father feels what we feel. Speaking of the children of Israel in Isaiah 63:9 (NLT), the prophet said, "In all their suffering he [God] also suffered, and he personally rescued them. In his love and mercy he redeemed them."

Remember the story of Lazarus in John 11? Jesus' friend Lazarus had died, and while his sisters, Mary and Martha, had sent for Jesus, He delayed answering the call. When He and the disciples finally arrived and approached the tomb, compassion overwhelmed our Lord. Verse 35 tells us, "Jesus wept." Being totally God, surely He knew that Lazarus would be raised from the dead, so why cry? Author Washington Irving may have accidentally or purposefully provided an answer. He wrote:

> There is a sacredness in tears. They are not the mark of weakness, but of power. They speak more eloquently than ten thousand tongues. They are the messengers of overwhelming grief, of deep contrition, and of unspeakable love.[26]

When I realized my mother was being beaten unmercifully, compassion engulfed me; I had to try to do something to help her. When you or I are hurting, compassion and love flows through our Lord. Jesus loves us so much that

He is willing to suffer with us. Because of His suffering and death, He identifies with His child and reaches out to provide comfort, support, and rescue. In Matthew 25:40, Jesus talked about giving aid to those with needs. He said, "Whatever you did for one of the least of these brothers and sisters of mine, you did for me" (NIV). Sometimes you and I come in contact with others who are "the least of these."

Sometimes we look in the mirror, and one of "the least" looks back at us. Disease has invaded; divorce has devastated; betrayal has ravaged us; death has shattered us; pain has overwhelmed us. In the midst of whatever has beset you and me, we have this assurance, "For it is the LORD your God who goes with you; He will not leave you or forsake you" (Deuteronomy 31:6 HCSB).

In the mid-1980s I was awaiting a flight at the airport in Rome when suddenly I spotted a short, stooped woman wearing a familiar robe sitting a few seats from me. I rose, approached her, and extended my hand. "My name is Mike Evans." Mother Teresa's dark eyes twinkled as she grasped my outstretched hand and said, "Mr. Evans, it is very nice to meet you."

I stammered a few words about my current mission to Israel, then collected myself and asked about her recent trip to the United States. I thought I would sympathize with her for returning to the suffering in India after enjoying the comforts of the States for a short time.

"No, no," she said with a sad smile. "It is in the United States that I am sad. I believe it is the poorest country on earth."

"But why?" I asked, stumbling in my attempt at small talk with this giant of faith.

"Ah," she said, "the United States is poor in spirit, and that is the worst kind of poverty."

In a land of wealth and opulence, we too often find ourselves filled with pain, devoid of true fulfillment and lasting contentment. Personal peace is fleeting, and achieving a fulfilling purpose for living seems to elude us. We struggle to discover our divine destiny, sometimes settling instead for complacency. We know that God loves us, but too often we're not sure how to fully experience that divine love.

Let me reassure you that Jehovah God truly loves us and will share our griefs and sorrows. Blogger Tara Lemieux posted the following story on "Mindfully Musing":

> Author and lecturer Leo Buscaglia once talked about a contest he was asked to judge. The purpose of the contest was to find the most caring child.

The winner was a four year old child whose next door neighbor was an elderly gentleman who had recently lost his wife.

> Upon seeing the man cry, the little boy went into the old gentleman's yard, climbed onto his lap, and just sat there.
>
> When his Mother asked what he had said to the neighbor, the little boy said, "Nothing, I just helped him cry."[27]

The abuse I suffered at the hands of my father caused untold suffering. As an adult, I found myself addicted to achievement, still struggling to gain my father's acceptance and approval and that of my heavenly Father as well. Do you see how our concept of our parents can affect our image of God? As an adolescent, I refused to read the books of the Old Testament simply because my image of God was so affected by my father's behavior toward his children. If we see our parents as cruel, hard, and punishing, we will tend to see God the same way; and we will respond to Him in anger and fear. You will find security when you find God, in whom you *can* believe.

You and I need to see God through the cross: a God who gives us security; a God who is so pure, so compassionate, and so loving, He is irresistible. We need a God who uses His power to empower us, not to dominate, and we need a God who offers us an abundant, fulfilling life, not just a bleak existence. There is only One who meets all those provisions: Jehovah-Eli—the Lord my God!

You and I must trust Him and learn to rely on His help and comfort. It takes a miracle of love and forgiveness for you and me to reach out to our Lord and allow Him to help us put the past behind.

Eventually, I forgave my father abundantly and unconditionally. During the last years of his life I was able to provide for him; but that's a story for another chapter.

SCRIPTURES ON GOD'S POWER

Colossians 1:16—For by him were all things created, that are in heaven, and that are in earth, visible and invisible, whether they be thrones, or dominions, or principalities, or powers: all things were created by him, and for him:

1 Chronicles 29:11—Thine, O Lord, is the greatness, and the power, and the glory, and the victory, and the majesty: for all that is in the heaven and in the earth is thine; thine is the kingdom, O Lord, and thou art exalted as head above all.

Exodus 14:14—The Lord shall fight for you, and ye shall hold your peace.

Psalm 28:7—The Lord is my strength and my shield; my heart trusted in him, and I am helped: therefore my heart greatly rejoiceth; and with my song will I praise him.

Proverbs 3:5–6—Trust in the Lord with all thine heart; and lean not unto thine own understanding. In all thy ways acknowledge him, and he shall direct thy paths.

Ephesians 1:19–21—And what is the exceeding greatness of his power to us-ward who believe, according to the working of his mighty power, which he wrought in Christ, when he raised him from the dead, and set him at his own right hand in the heavenly places, Far above all principality, and power, and might, and dominion, and every name that is named, not only in this world, but also in that which is to come:

11

A BRIGHT LIGHT IN A DARK ROOM

(YOU ARE GOD'S CHILD)

Battered, beaten, bruised, and bloody, I lay on the floor of my bedroom. Listening intently, my heart beat rapidly for fear that my father would return to finish what he had started. My life had no purpose, no meaning. Was I always to be a punching bag for Dad's huge fists? It was then I prayed, "Why was I born?"

As quickly as I had whispered those words, the room was flooded with a light so bright it blinded me. It reminded me of a giant spotlight. My terror was uncontrollable. I thought Dad had come back to finish the job. He was going to beat me to death, and this time I would not escape. I heard a noise that sounded like a wounded puppy's whine and realized the sound was coming from my own throat.

My first thought was to crawl under the bed to protect myself, certain I was about to be the victim of his steel-toed boots.

I covered my face with my hands and closed my eyes as tightly as I could squeeze them. After what seemed like an eon, I realized there was no other sound in the room. My father would surely have already been screaming and cursing. Now there was only a brilliant light. I slowly spread my fingers and eased my eyes open as imperceptibly as possible, hoping to see an empty room.

That light changed my life forever.

I didn't know at the time that there was a place called Carlsbad Caverns in New Mexico. It is, however, a perfect example of what the entrance of light can achieve in a life. At one point during the tour of the cavern, the guide asks everyone to sit. The lights are then turned off in the huge underground room for a few moments; the darkness is complete. You literally cannot see your hand held in front of your face. When the tourists begin to fear they will never see the light of day again, one tiny light dispels the blackness and brings a sense of security in the depths of darkness. This is exactly how the light in my bedroom reached inside the darkness of my life and changed me from within.

Galatians 3:26–29 (NLT) reminds us who we are:

> For you are all children of God through faith in Christ Jesus. And all who have been united with Christ in baptism have put on Christ, like putting on new clothes. There is no longer Jew or Gentile, slave or free, male and female. For you are all one in Christ Jesus. And now that you belong to Christ, you are the true children of Abraham. You are his heirs, and God's promise to Abraham belongs to you.

There on my bedroom floor, I was about to discover who I really was—a beloved child of God, valued, treasured, priceless. This revelation was joy unspeakable. It is in Christ that we live and move and have our being. Mark Stephenson, director of Disability Concerns for the Christian Reformed Church, wrote of a young man who believed himself unworthy:

> Writer and preacher Fred Craddock tells about a new preacher who was greeting his congregation after a worship service. As one boy tried to sneak away, the preacher called

out, "Hey, whose boy are you?" The boy froze. It was the last thing he wanted to be asked. The boy had been born to a mother who wasn't married, so in that day and in that place he had a big strike against him. People gave him a label that spat shame on him. The kids threw that label at him at school. The townspeople whispered it about him everywhere. The boy's mother had wanted him to go to Sunday school, but the people at the church asked him not to come back because they said he was a bad influence. Though he didn't return to Sunday school, he wanted to check out the new preacher. As he snuck away after the service, the preacher saw him and asked him the terrible question. Before the boy answered, the preacher said, "I know who you are. I can see the family resemblance." Then everyone froze until the preacher continued: "You're a child of God!"[28]

That, I believe, is what God wants us to understand above all else. Although *we* may believe we are unworthy of His great love, we are His children. First John 3:1 reminds us:

"See what great love the Father has for us that He would call us His children" (NIV). John doesn't say that we are children of God because we say the correct things, pray the lengthiest prayer, or have been a Christian for forty years. We don't have to prove moment by moment how patient we are, how much we have donated to the church, or how pious we are. I have news for you: Doing those things will not secure your place in heaven. Only one thing will do that: the blood of Jesus Christ His Son that cleanses us from all sin (see 1 John 1:7 KJV).

A few readers will remember a time before electricity was in their home with the widespread use of lightbulbs—the days of candle power or oil lamps. Today, most of us tend to take for granted the ability to walk into a room, flip a switch, and have instant light at our disposal. That is, until a power failure. The lights are out, and we know it; yet we still walk into a room and feel silly when we reach for the switch or try to turn on the television. How we rejoice when, in the middle of the night, the electricity is restored and lights blink on in every room! No matter how bright those lights, they cannot compare to the light that filled my room when I was just eleven years old. It was like looking at the sun, but it didn't hurt my eyes. Instead, it produced a warm glow that filled the very core of my being.

The light revealed that my father was no longer standing over me, poised to inflict more pain. I could no longer hear his threats; I could no longer see the rage on his blotchy face. Yes, Someone was there, but the presence was not threatening; it was reassuring. Without being aware of having made that assessment, I felt safe and secure.

Where there had been agonizing pain and paralyzing fear, now there was a supernatural energy. In a sermon by Phillips Brooks, once the rector of Boston's famed Trinity Church, light was aptly described:

> When the sun rose this morning it found the world in darkness, torpid and heavy and asleep, with powers all wrapped up in sluggishness; with life that was hardly better or more alive than death.
>
> The sun found this great sleeping world and woke it. It bade it to be itself. It quickened every slow and sluggish faculty. It called to the dull streams and said, 'Be quick;' to the dull birds and bade them sing; to the dull fields and made them grow; to the dull men and bade them think and talk and work.

> It flashed electric invitations to the whole mass of sleeping power which really was the world and summoned it to action. It did not make the world. It did not start another set of processes unlike those which had been sluggishly moving in the darkness. It poured strength into the essential processes which belonged to the very nature of the earth. It glorified, intensified, fulfilled the earth.[29]

Before the light infiltrated my room, I was depressed, demoralized, and distressed. I was about to discover for myself the truth in Ephesians 5:8–9 (NLT):

> For once you were full of darkness, but now you have light from the Lord. So live as people of light! For this light within you produces only what is good and right and true.

Have you discovered the light of God's salvation, His grace, His Word? Lutheran pastor Joel Pankow preached a sermon titled, "God's Light Shines in the Darkness." He told his listeners:

> God, who said, "Let light shine out of darkness," made his light shine in our hearts to

give us the light of the knowledge of the glory of God in the face of Christ. Darkness is, in an ironic way, the best place for the light to shine. When a light shines in the light it tends to dilute the light. But when a light shines in the darkness it is appreciated and used. Imagine the most dark and disturbing periods in your life that you try to repress and forget; what if Jesus could fill that memory with His love and forgiveness? This is what He wants to do. It is what the light is for. He doesn't want any darkness.[30]

Are there areas in your life that need to be illuminated by the light of God's love and grace? Proverbs 16:15 reminds us, "In the light of the king's countenance is life" (KJV). Beaten within an inch of my existence, I found that life on the floor of my bedroom on Pascoe Road in Springfield, Massachusetts.

We need only to allow God—His Light, His word, His truth—to enter our hearts and we find that God provides enough for us to withstand all that we face. We may want more, but we can only handle so much. Second, light provides direction and saves lives:

A missionary home on furlough told of a simple act of his by which he unconsciously saved another's life. He was onboard a ship and when in his berth one dark night, he heard that cry—so awful at sea—"Man overboard." He arose at once. . . took his swinging lamp from its bracket, and held it at the window in his cabin.

He could see nothing; but, the next morning, he was told that the flash of his lamp through the port showed to those on the deck the missing man clinging to a rope. He could hardly have held on another minute. The light of the lamp shone just in time to save the man's life.[31]

The writer of Hebrews reminds us that we can "go right into the presence of God with sincere hearts fully trusting him" (Hebrews 10:22 NLT). Reach out to God with your whole heart! You will find light, joy, and hope, not darkness and despair. It is a step you will never regret, for He is light and in Him is no darkness (see 1 John 1:5).

SCRIPTURES ON GOD'S PLEASURE IN HIS CHILDREN

Psalm 5:3–4—My voice You shall hear in the morning, O Lord; in the morning I will direct it to You, and I will look up. For You are not a God who takes pleasure in wickedness, nor shall evil dwell with You.

Psalm 35:27—Let them shout for joy and be glad, who favor my righteous cause; and let them say continually, "Let the Lord be magnified, who has pleasure in the prosperity of His servant."

Psalm 103:21–22—Bless the Lord, all you His hosts, You ministers of His, who do His pleasure. Bless the Lord, all His works, in all places of His dominion. Bless the Lord, O my soul!

Psalm 147:11—The Lord takes pleasure in those who fear Him, in those who hope in His mercy.

Psalm 149:4—For the Lord takes pleasure in His people; He will beautify the humble with salvation.

Philippians 2:12–13—Therefore, my beloved, as you have always obeyed, not as in my presence only, but now much more in my absence, work out your own salvation with fear and trembling; for it is God who works in you both to will and to do for His good pleasure.

2 Thessalonians 1:11–12—Therefore we also pray always for you that our God would count you worthy of this calling, and fulfill all the good pleasure of His goodness and the work of faith with power, that the name of our Lord Jesus Christ may be glorified in you, and you in Him, according to the grace of our God and the Lord Jesus Christ.

12

NAIL SCARS AND SMILING EYES

(JESUS IS MAJESTIC IN HIS GREATNESS)

There I was, lying on my bedroom floor in physical and mental anguish. Beneath my cheek was a pool of vomit mixed with my own blood. Where there had been darkness there was now light—brilliant white light. Nothing escaped its rays. I clapped my hands over my eyes to block its intensity, but still it seeped between my tightly closed fingers. Slowly, I eased those fingers apart and raised my head slightly, expecting to see the anger-deformed face of my earthly father.

Terror gripped me as I saw two arms reaching for me. With almost supernatural clarity, I realized those were not Dad's hands. As I looked more closely, I realized that in the center of each wrist was a horrific, jagged scar. It appeared as though each one had been snagged and then ripped open on a large spike. Slowly it dawned on me that I had seen pictures of those scars on the leaflets we had been given in Sunday school on Easter. Surely I was hallucinating; or had I gone completely crazy? Jesus would not—could not—be in my bedroom. I was having a complete nervous breakdown. That explained it.

Something else plagued me: Where had my fear gone? Maybe Dad had achieved his purpose—to kill the "bastard" in his house. How could the vision I was seeing be possible otherwise? How else could I experience such power and peace unless I was dead?

My disbelieving eyes followed those arms up and up until I could see the source of the light. I saw standing there in my bedroom the Lord Jesus Christ. He was either clothed in light or in the most brilliant white imaginable—whiter than fresh snow; whiter than the clouds that floated in a sun-filled sky; whiter than anything I had ever seen. Draped from His shoulder to His waist was a deep purple cloth—more purple than the heavens at sunset.

As I lifted my head to look at His face, I was instantly drawn to His eyes. They were smiling, happy eyes filled with every color of the rainbow, and they were fixed on me. It was like looking into an illuminated bowl of the world's most highly prized jewels. I felt as if I could see through them and beyond to heaven and the promise of eternal peace. They were like magnets drawing me into their depths. Keeping His arms outstretched, He looked at me with such an expression of love.

Christian singer Holly Starr penned the words of the song "Through My Father's Eyes." She wrote:

> I know I'm not the only one who's ever cried
> for help,
> And Jesus did for me what I
> could not do myself.
> He changed my life by changing my mind.
> He healed all that was broken inside.
> I'm loving what I can see with
> His spirit alive in me.
> I'm finding beauty for the first time
> Looking through my Father's eyes.[32]

When *I* looked in the mirror, I saw myself through my earthly father's eyes—a bastard, a moron, unloved and unlovable. I was invisible until the moment Dad deemed I had committed what he thought was some unpardonable sin. Then the extension cord, used like a whip, would find my back, legs, and buttocks in painful retribution.

In Luke chapter seven, Jesus had been invited to dinner at the home of Simon, a Pharisee—one who strictly observed the law of Moses. Perhaps he was curious about this "Rabbi" from Galilee. Traditionally, dinner was eaten either in the courtyard of the home or in a side room. This meeting likely took place in the courtyard, for it was there that the uninvited could enter and learn from the teachings of the Rabbi. Simon's attention was captured by Jesus when He was approached by a woman in the crowd.

In this story, she is nameless and of little consequence to the other guests—until she approaches the Rabbi. Had you been there, her actions might have drawn an audible gasp from the bystanders. It was likely that she was a woman of ill repute; the Scriptures only say that she had "lived a sinful life." It may be that Simon totally ignored her presence; she was not worthy to be in his august presence.

The woman approached Jesus from behind as he reclined on a couch to eat. Is it possible that she could have met the Rabbi before and had seen His love and grace extended? She may have come to express her love and gratitude for His kindness and compassion. She was so overcome with emotion that she began to wail and sob. As copious tears fell from her eyes, they landed on the feet of the Rabbi. She washed His dusty feet with her tears and then dried them with her hair. As she ministered to our Lord, she repeatedly kissed His feet. An alabaster box that held highly prized perfume was opened and with its fragrant oil she anointed the feet of Jesus.

I am reminded of a line from an old song by Ira Stanphill, "He washed my eyes with tears that I might see the glory of Himself revealed to me."[33] Jesus saw the woman as a beloved child, not an object to be bought and sold or callously dismissed. He saw her through smiling eyes as a daughter to be cherished.

Conversely, Simon saw her as an intrusion, an outcast, not worthy of acknowledgment, and upbraided his guest. Verse 39 shows us Simon's response—one of arrogance and scorn:

> When the Pharisee who had invited him saw this, he said to himself, "If this man were a prophet, he would know who is touching him and what kind of woman she is—that she is a sinner." (NIV)

Jesus immediately and directly addressed the Pharisee's misconceptions. He asked a very pointed question: "Do you even see this woman? Take a good look, Simon. See her heart. See her love. See her devotion. Do you see what I see?"

When I looked into the eyes of Jesus all those years ago, I saw a new me—loved, wanted, precious, valuable. There was no condemnation in those sparkling, smiling eyes. I had never seen that phenomenon in my youth.

Simon seems not to realize in whose presence he sat. It was not he who garnered Jesus' favor; it was the woman who offered nothing but praise and adoration. Simon had offered Him no water to wash the dust of the road from His feet—a most common courtesy in that day. The woman with her tears did what Simon did not: She offered him hospitality and respect. The Pharisee should have been highly embarrassed at the discourteous treatment of an invited guest. Simon gave Jesus no kiss of greeting, yet the woman kissed his feet repeatedly. Simon failed to anoint Jesus' head with oil—another sign of civility. The woman poured her alabaster bottle of oil on His feet.

Nothing she offered or sacrificed went unnoticed by our Lord. Jesus then informed Simon that the woman's sins had been forgiven—all of them, regardless of number or severity. In Jesus' smiling eyes, I, too, saw the promise of hope. They seemed to mirror for me the promise in Jeremiah 29:11 (NIV):

> "For I know the plans I have for you," declares the LORD, "plans to prosper you and

not to harm you, plans to give you hope and a future."

God has a plan for you, and not just *any* plan. It is one that will bring you hope and a future. In this verse, the word for "you" indicates plurality; it is for everyone who is reading these words at this moment. God has a plan for your future. He wants you to walk in His footsteps, listen to His voice, read His Word, and walk uprightly before Him. He does not *plan* harm for you; rather, that you prosper. John wrote in the third book of his epistles, chapter 1, verse 2, "Beloved, I pray that you may prosper in all things and be in health, just as your soul prospers" (NKJV).

Jeremiah 29:12 assures that not only does God have a plan for our lives, He also wants us to call on Him in times of need: "Then you will call upon Me and go and pray to Me, and I will listen to you."

What a precious promise! When we call upon Him, God has vowed to listen and not just half-heartedly; He pays complete attention to our cry. You and I are not necessarily "hard of hearing." Too often we are "hard of listening." Not so with our heavenly Father. What this verse reveals is that God pays personal attention to you and me. No longer do we need an earthly high priest or a go-between. Nor does He require the sacrifice of a lamb. No, because of the death of Jesus on the cross, we can enter the holy of holies and lay down our requests at His feet. It is not necessary to travel to Jerusalem to the temple. Why? First Corinthians 6:19 (NIV) answers that question:

> Do you not know that your bodies are temples of the Holy Spirit, who is in you, whom you have received from God? You are not your own.

We are assured that not only will God listen to us when we call on Him but He will also reveal the plan He has for our lives. We have these great and precious promises.

God desires that His beloved children have a prosperous journey of faith, be in spiritual health, and above all devote time to the study of the Word. These are the promises I saw in the eyes of Jesus that long-ago night—even before He opened His mouth to speak life-changing words into my life.

Call on Him today; let Him show you the wonderful design He has for you.

SCRIPTURES ON GOD'S MAJESTY

1 Chronicles 29:11—Thine, O Lord, is the greatness, and the power, and the glory, and the victory, and the majesty: for all that is in the heaven and in the earth is thine; thine is the kingdom, O LORD, and thou art exalted as head above all.

1 Chronicles 29:25—And the Lord magnified Solomon exceedingly in the sight of all Israel, and bestowed upon him such royal majesty as had not been on any king before him in Israel.

Psalm 29:4—The voice of the Lord is powerful; the voice of the Lord is full of majesty.

Psalm 45:4—And in thy majesty ride prosperously because of truth and meekness and righteousness; and thy right hand shall teach thee terrible things.

Psalm 93:1—The Lord reigneth, he is clothed with majesty; the Lord is clothed with strength, wherewith he hath girded himself: the world also is stablished, that it cannot be moved.

Psalm 96:6—Honour and majesty are before him: strength and beauty are in his sanctuary.

Psalm 104:1—Bless the Lord, O my soul. O Lord my God, thou art very great; thou art clothed with honour and majesty.

Psalm 145:5—I will speak of the glorious honour of thy majesty, and of thy wondrous works.

Micah 5:4—And he shall stand and feed in the strength of the Lord, in the majesty of the name of the Lord his God; and they shall abide: for now shall he be great unto the ends of the earth.

Hebrews 1:3—Who being the brightness of his glory, and the express image of his person, and upholding all things by the word of his power, when he had by himself purged our sins, sat down on the right hand of the Majesty on high:

13

HE CALLED ME "SON"

(YOU ARE HIS CHILD; HE CREATED YOU FOR A PURPOSE)

It had barely registered in my adolescent mind that the glorious Personage in my room was Jesus—the Light of the World, the Alpha and Omega—as He continued to stand with arms outstretched toward me. I was mesmerized by His presence alone, but then He spoke. With a look that melted my heart, He gently and lovingly spoke a word that I had never heard. Jesus called me "son." It was the first time anyone had ever used that word associated with me, and it was life-giving. Songwriter Charles A. Miles penned the words to the beautiful hymn "In the Garden." He wrote:

> He speaks and the sound of His voice
> Is so sweet the birds hush their singing,
> And the melody that He gave to me
> Within my heart is ringing.[34]

The sound of His voice immediately calmed my fears; it was like a healing balm to my wounded soul and spirit. *"Son."* It was said so gently and with such love and respect for me—for *me!*—that I felt as if my heart would melt. The word echoed again and again through my weary spirit. Like King David, I could say, "How sweet your words taste to me; they are sweeter than honey" (Psalm 119:103 NLT).

Perhaps you are thinking, *It's wonderful that Jesus appeared and spoke to you, but I haven't had that experience. I've never heard the voice of God!* That was one of my greatest life challenges after seeing Jesus face-to-face and hearing Him speak to me as a child: I wanted to hear His voice once more. Through prayer and Bible study, I did learn how to hear the voice of God again and again, and the results have been just as radical as that first encounter.

Wait for Him to speak His Word into your life, and don't allow anyone to talk you out of your blessing, your favor. I have trusted Him with my life and my ministry. I have learned that sometimes He speaks through His Word, sometimes through godly men and women, and sometimes through circumstances. And then there are the times He speaks directly into your spirit.

It is reminiscent of the plight of the world during Noah's time as told at length in Genesis:

> The Lord saw how great the wickedness
> of the human race had become on the earth,
> and that every inclination of the thoughts of
> the human heart was only evil all the time.
> The Lord regretted that he had made human
> beings on the earth, and his heart was deeply
> troubled. (Genesis 6:5–6 NIV)

Everywhere the Creator looked, evil reigned. Verse seven says God repented that He had made Man—God could see that mankind was limited only by his imagination. All seemed to be lost; the only thing left was to destroy it all. But wait! There *was* one righteous man among the unrighteous. His name was Noah, and he found favor in God's eyes.

The Statler Brothers, a country singing group, told the story of Noah in their best-selling song "Noah Found Grace in the Eyes of the Lord":

> So the Lord came down to look around a spell
> And there He found Noah behavin' mighty well
> And that is the reason the Scriptures record
> Noah found grace in the eyes of the Lord.[35]

One day as Noah was going about his business God spoke and extended grace to him and his family. Jehovah warned Noah that He was about to intervene. Was that righteous man as grieved about the lawlessness on earth as God was? Had Noah spent time in fellowship with the Creator, seeking His face and His will? No matter the reason, Noah had captured God's attention. Because of Noah's righteousness, God determined not to just wipe the slate clean and start over with a new creation.

God brought forth a plan, and it involved obedience. He began to share with Noah that he had been appointed to complete a special assignment—building an ark. Now, Noah probably had no idea what an "ark" was, yet he was willing to follow God's directions. Then the Master Architect gave His builder the blueprint for the ark: It was to be 300 cubits long by 50 cubits wide by 30 cubits high. (That translates to about 450 feet long by 75 feet wide by 45 feet high.) The ark would have three floors to house the creatures that God commanded should be loaded in the structure. Upon its completion, it was to be coated inside and out with pitch.

In the Hebrew language, the word for *pitch* means "to cover over, to atone for sin." The ark was designed to cover Noah and his family. God's judgment was rampant over the face of the earth, but inside the ark, Noah and his family were safe. When Christ died on the cross, He provided the pitch—the blood that covers our sin. The Believer protected by the blood of Christ—pitch—is safe from the wrath of God.

Noah's obedience would ensure him, his wife, his three sons—Shem, Ham, and Japheth, and their wives—a place of safety. They would be spared the destruction that was about to rain down—literally—upon the earth. As he worked on the vessel, Noah preached righteousness to any who would listen. The response: ridicule, derision, mockery, and scorn.

Bible scholars tell us that before the time of Noah, it had never rained on the earth. The faithless were unable to accept by faith that God would fulfill His declaration—whether or not they knew what "rain" was. They had the choice to believe or reject, and the overwhelming majority chose disbelief and rejection.

Noah and his family obeyed the voice of God, the direction to enter the ark through its lone door and be saved. Noah must have been quite an example to his sons who worked alongside their father to fulfill God's directive. He obeyed despite the harassment. He had followed the instructions to gather the animals as outlined and see them safely inside. He had gathered food for the preservation of his family, all the while warning of the impending disaster. He was completely faithful to Jehovah—the characteristic of a true servant of God.

Simply stated: Noah believed God and, like Abraham after him, God "counted it to him for righteousness" (Genesis 15:6 KJV). And God blessed Noah abundantly. Because of his faith and obedience, Noah received a rich reward from the Creator. He enjoyed intimacy with Jehovah. They walked and talked together. God laid out the plan and Noah followed it to the letter. Faith coupled with obedience cannot be undervalued. These are qualities that must infuse the spiritual life of a Christian in order to enjoy the favor of God.

From that first encounter as a child, I began to learn that God did, indeed, speak to me—and everything He said, no matter the delivery method, was of great importance. It was up to me to stay tuned to His wavelength. It was up to me, as it is with you, to turn off the television, the radio, the iPad, or my various devices and listen! The appropriate response when God speaks—however that may be manifest—is, "Speak, Lord, for your servant is listening."

To hear God, you and I must listen with our entire being: mind, soul, and body. It is difficult to hear his voice over the cacophony that constantly surrounds us. Parents sleep with one ear tuned to the nursery, waiting for a babe's cry in the night. As Believers, we must walk with our ears totally tuned to the Father so that we can hear that still, small voice that calls to us above the frenzied crowds.

What, then, do you think God might wish to say to us once He has our attention? Perhaps, as He did me, He would call you "son" or "daughter." He might tell you that He had been searching for you as He did the lost sheep or the prodigal son. Our Lord could possibly warn you that there was danger ahead and you needed to change direction. John, the Beloved, wrote in chapter 3, verses 16–17 (KJV):

> For God so loved the world, that he gave his only begotten Son, that whosoever believeth in him should not perish, but have everlasting life. For God sent not his Son into the world to condemn the world; but that the world through him might be saved.

Our loving heavenly Father could let you and me know that we can be overcomers through Him; if we follow in His footsteps, He will lead us in the way we are to go. Then He will whisper, "Lo, I am with you always, even unto the end of the world" (Matthew 28:20b KJV).

That great orator and preacher Charles Spurgeon said:

> Having once discerned the voice of God, obey without question. If you have to stand alone and nobody will befriend you, stand alone.... [36]

God calls the humble and obedient to fulfill His mission. His power is made perfect in your weakness. Only with the realization that you can do nothing without Jehovah are you then ready to be used by Him.

Jehovah has called us to live our lives like someone formed in His image. He wants us to know that we, His creation, are valuable and significant to Him. Ephesians 2:10 (KJV) reveals:

> For we are his workmanship, created in Christ Jesus unto good works, which God hath before ordained that we should walk in them.

What shapes our lives so that we can be more like Him? We are honed through the study of the Word, through prayer, through praise, and through worship. And believe it or not our trials and tribulations cause us to grow by sharing our faith, by reaching out to others if we turn them over to Him. You and I must realize that we are not self-sufficient; we depend solely on Him. He bids us look up and live. In 1922, Helen Lemmel, singer and daughter of a Methodist minister, wrote a beautiful hymn, "Turn Your Eyes Upon Jesus." She sang:

O soul, are you weary and troubled?

No light in the darkness you see?

There's light for a look at the Savior,

And life more abundant and free!

Turn your eyes upon Jesus,

Look full in His wonderful face,

And the things of earth will grow strangely dim,

In the light of His glory and grace.

My encounter with Jesus has led me down some amazing and unbelievable paths, but the first step was to look up at Him and then to hear Him call me "son."

SCRIPTURES OF GOD'S PURPOSE

Exodus 9:16—But I have raised you up for this very purpose, that I might show you my power and that my name might be proclaimed in all the earth.

Job 42:2—I know that you can do all things; no purpose of yours can be thwarted.

Proverbs 19:21—Many are the plans in a person's heart, but it is the Lord's purpose that prevails.

Proverbs 20:5—The purposes of a person's heart are deep waters, but one who has insight draws them out.

Philippians 2:12-13—Therefore, my dear friends, as you have always obeyed—not only in my presence, but now much more in my absence—continue to work out your salvation with fear and trembling, for it is God who works in you to will and to act in order to fulfill his good purpose.

Romans 8:28—And we know that in all things God works for the good of those who love him, who have been called according to his purpose.

2 Timothy 1:9—He has saved us and called us to a holy life—not because of anything we have done but because of his own purpose and grace.

14

"I LOVE YOU!"

(GOD TRULY LOVES YOU)

There I was, lying on the floor of my bedroom, surrounded by the most brilliant light imaginable. Suddenly I heard the voice of Jesus speak to me. First, He called me "son." Then He whispered three words that had, sadly, been missing from my life: "I love you." Me, Michael Evans, aka "Moron," was loved by the Lord of all creation! Someone really *did* love me. What joy! I felt as if I'd just escaped a death sentence and was free. That statement alone was enough to sustain me for the rest of my life.

I am reminded of Kurt Kaiser's beautiful hymn, "O How He Loves You and Me," when he penned these words of praise:

> O how He loves you and me,
> O how He loves you and me,

> He gave His life, what more could He give?
>
> O how He loves you,
>
> O how He loves me,
>
> O how He loves you and me.[37]

My reality was: my father hated me, and my mother suffered because of me. All I knew was Dad's warped version of Christianity: booze on Friday, beatings on Saturday, church on Sunday. My dad's favorite Bible verse must have been Proverbs 23:14: "You shall beat him with a rod, and deliver his soul from hell." He paraphrased that as "Spare the rod, spoil the child." There were no spoiled children in his house—only abused ones. He had never given me one word of affirmation. Not once had I heard "I love you" from the lips of my earthly father. My mother's sister, Ginger, could say those words, but even my mother couldn't seem to utter them unless I first said them to her. My father was totally incapable of speaking those words.

One woman who had experienced such a relationship with her father wrote a letter describing what it was like to be the child of an angry parent who both loves and hurts:

> I loved and adored you so much, but I'd tremble with fear when you were angry with me. I did everything to try to please you, but

no accomplishment ever seemed enough for you. You compared me to all my friends. This one was prettier, that one was smarter. Then if I achieved something, you belittled it. If I didn't achieve what you wanted me to, you called me a failure. You constantly humiliated and degraded me in front of others. I never knew what you wanted from me.[38]

Bruises and lacerations on the spirit of a child can hurt just as much as welts and cuts on the physical body. And often the pain and scars last a lot longer, even a lifetime.

Having grown up not feeling particularly loved by anyone, it was a stunning revelation in my bedroom that dark night to realize that I *was* loved, a feeling I never wanted to lose. Just as God wanted me to know I was loved, so Paul wrote to the Ephesians:

> That you, being rooted and grounded in love, may be able to comprehend with all the saints what is the width and length and depth and height—to know the love of Christ which passes knowledge; that you may be filled with all the fullness of God. (Ephesians 3:17b–19 NKJV)

Former pastor and motivational speaker Jeff VanVonderen wrote:

> The degree to which people are convinced that they are loved unconditionally; that they are valuable, gifted and special; and that they are not alone to face life's struggles is the same degree to which they will be able to love, serve and build others up. The degree to which individuals are not convinced of these things is the same degree to which they will function out of emptiness and shame.[39]

When we dissect the Scriptures from Ephesians 3, we find the word *rooted*. David painted a picture in Psalm 1:3 of someone who is "like a tree planted by streams of water, which yields its fruit in season and whose leaf does not wither—whatever they do prospers" (NIV). When you and I are rooted and grounded in God, we find nourishment in Him, in His Word, and in His great love.

Paul also tells us we are like a building that is built on bedrock. In Matthew 7:24–25 (NKJV), Jesus told His followers:

"Therefore whoever hears these sayings of Mine, and does them, I will liken him to a wise man who built his house on the rock: and the rain descended, the floods came, and the winds blew and beat on that house; and it did not fall, for it was founded on the rock."

In 1834, British hymn writer Edward Mote penned the immortal words, "On Christ the solid Rock I stand, all other ground is sinking sand, all other ground is sinking sand."[40] God's love is immoveable, unshakable, and eternal.

Oh, how you and I crave the kind of love that Paul tries to paint for us—a love that is a net to catch us when we stumble and fall. We want to be precious to someone—treasured and respected. Our hearts are hungry to experience that abundant love.

What a wonderful picture of strength and grace! You and I stand not on sand but on a foundation established by the Master Builder. We have been established, rooted, and grounded by the powerful agape love of the Holy Spirit.

What does that mean? *Agape* is the Greek word that means: "the highest form of love, [especially brotherly love,] charity; the love of God for man and of man for God."[41] The ultimate expression of Agape love was nailed to a cross for my sins and yours. God gave His only Son so that you and I could have a pathway to Him and saving grace. Never doubt that you are loved by God. That perfect love is the most elementary spiritual detail. It is as real as the air we breathe, and just as necessary to our life in the Spirit.

When did this marvelous love for us begin? Paul reveals the answer in Ephesians 1:3–6 (NKJV):

> Blessed be the God and Father of our Lord Jesus Christ, who has blessed us with every spiritual blessing in the heavenly places in Christ, just as He chose us in Him before the foundation of the world, that we should be holy and without blame before Him in love, having predestined us to adoption as sons by Jesus Christ to Himself, according to the good pleasure of His will, to the praise of the glory of His grace, by which He made us accepted in the Beloved.

Before the foundation of the world was ever laid, before the first star was flung into space, or the sun, moon, and planets were ever launched in the heavens, God loved you and me.

What can separate us from the love of God? Nothing—no single thing! The writer of Romans expounded on this in chapter 8:

> For I am convinced that neither death nor life, neither angels nor demons, neither the present nor the future, nor any powers, neither height nor depth, nor anything else in all creation, will be able to separate us from the love of God that is in Christ Jesus our Lord. (Romans 8:38–39 NIV)

In his book *Grace for the Moment,* Max Lucado addresses God's love:

> God loves you just the way you are. If you think his love for you would be stronger if your faith were, you are wrong. If you think his love would be deeper if your thoughts were, wrong again. Don't confuse God's love with the love of people. The love of people often increases with performance and decreases with mistakes. Not so with God's love. He loves you right where you are.[42]

At the age of eleven, I had no idea that those three words, *"I love you,"* would launch my life in Christ. Like the apostle Paul, who encountered Christ on the road to Damascus, my life changed dramatically. Before I met Jesus in my bedroom, I was: abused, miserable, depressed, and disheartened. Before his conversion, Paul (then Saul) was: radical, fanatical, egotistical, determined, uncompromising, and arrogant—the exact opposite of the humble servant of Christ. What a change was wrought in Saul as he stalked toward Damascus on his mission! He lost Self in the light of God's love and grace, changed his name to Paul, and his entire demeanor was transformed:

> I became a servant of this gospel by the gift of God's grace given me through the working of his power. Although I am less than the least of all the Lord's people, this grace was given me: to preach to the Gentiles the boundless riches of Christ. (Ephesians 3:7–8 NIV)

Paul turned from being a fearsome adversary to the cause of Christ to becoming "less than the least." This phrase truly portrays Paul's conversion; it was not a garment that he put on when convenient in order to impress others.

In his own judgment, Paul was on a lower level than all the saints who were serving Christ in their daily and dangerous determination to walk in His light. There is no reason or grounds to question Paul's genuineness in his own assessment. He had, after his encounter on the road to Damascus, become a deeply, profoundly humble man.

For most of my early adult years I strove for perfection and performance in a painful, desperate effort to gain my father's approval and acceptance. Shamed by the rejection and degrading abuse I had received growing up and intimidated by my lack of education, I struggled to prove to my father and to myself that I was a person of value and worth, not a piece of garbage.

As did the seven-year-old boy from long ago who had proudly shown his father the shiny jackknife he had found in the snow, the adult me still longed to see a flash of pride on my father's face. Hungry for some small nod of approval or just a faint smile of acceptance, I had proudly paraded my every hard-won accomplishment before him.

As I lay in a cardiology ward at the age of thirty-two, God brought me face-to-face with my broken places. Tormented by fears of failure, ridicule, and rejection, I had tried to be perfect in every area of my life: The perfect father, husband, even the perfect evangelist. The pressure of striving to be perfect absolutely broke me physically because there's no one perfect except Jesus. I worked so hard to keep up a front of perfection, but the shabby barrier of patched-up disappointments masked my weaknesses and carefully covered failures I had erected between myself and everyone else. All the music of healing and joy had been shut out of my life.

As I lay in that hospital bed suffering from tachycardia, God brought me to the place where I could be honest with myself and Him. I finally realized that I had to stop suppressing and hiding the past. As I admitted and accepted all my broken places and exposed them first to God and then to my dad, the Spirit of God was released to perform a supernatural healing in my life and in the life of my father, as well.

If you are experiencing pain today because of rejection and past hurts, please don't suppress them any longer. Take all your pain to Jesus. He understands. He allowed His body to be broken so that we, who are also broken, could be made whole.

It would be several years before I understood the full impact of what had happened in my bedroom that bleak night. As I have dared to share the story of the atrocities I once endured, the story of a frightened, rejected little boy's terrible suffering is being told here to bring healing and hope to hurting people—people struggling for perfection, performance, and praise; people with plastic smiles on their faces and gaping holes in their souls; people of all ages and from every strata of society who so desperately need to hear that a Savior with smiling eyes and nail scars loves, accepts, and values them, and that He has a wonderful plan for their lives.

SCRIPTURES ON BEING ROOTED IN CHRIST

Jeremiah 17:7–8—Blessed is the man that trusteth in the Lord, and whose hope the Lord is.

Colossians 2:6–7—As ye have therefore received Christ Jesus the Lord, so walk ye in him:

Psalm 1:3—And he shall be like a tree planted by the rivers of water, that bringeth forth his fruit in his season; his leaf also shall not wither; and whatsoever he doeth shall prosper.

Ephesians 3:16–19—That he would grant you, according to the riches of his glory, to be strengthened with might by his Spirit in the inner man;

Mark 4:17—And have no root in themselves, and so endure but for a time: afterward, when affliction or persecution ariseth for the word's sake, immediately they are offended.

Hebrews 12:15—Looking diligently lest any man fail of the grace of God; lest any root of bitterness springing up trouble you, and thereby many be defiled;

Romans 11:16—For if the firstfruit be holy, the lump is also holy: and if the root be holy, so are the branches.

Isaiah 11:10—And in that day there shall be a root of Jesse, which shall stand for an ensign of the people; to it shall the Gentiles seek: and his rest shall be glorious.

15

"I HAVE A GREAT PLAN FOR YOUR LIFE"

(GOD'S PLAN FOR YOU)

"I love you." Those words flooded by mind, ran unrestrained through my soul, and encouraged my spirit like nothing else in my life ever had. Someone really did love me. What joy! I felt as if I'd just escaped a death sentence and had been set free. That statement alone would be enough to sustain me for the rest of my life. But then Jesus continued, "I have a great plan for your life." The power and presence of Jesus was like a holy fire igniting my soul. I had a purpose! God had something for me—Michael Evans—to do.

Then there was silence. I am sure only a few seconds had passed, but it felt like an eternity. I closed my eyes, and tears slid slowly down my face. I was consumed with an inexplicable joy. Eventually I realized that the light had departed but the overwhelming warmth remained. He was gone from my room but not from my being, not from my heart. In my own childlike way, I promised Him that I would serve Him, would keep myself pure, and would not take His name in vain.

That night would prove to be the most glorious of my life—a night never to be forgotten. Even today I can close my eyes and still feel the joy and peace of the awesome presence of Jesus. I had truly been gloriously born again.

I finally drifted off to sleep, battered, bruised, broken, but not bereft. Jesus was with me. When I awoke the next morning, I stretched, rolled out of bed, and abruptly remembered the beating I had endured the night before. At first, I thought it had been a nightmare. Then I remembered the visitation from Jesus and began to cry with joy. I thought, *If that was a dream, what a glorious dream it was!*

Tentatively I stretched again. No pain! My arms that had been too painful to move the night before now swung freely. Slowly I turned and made my way down the hall to the bathroom. I opened the door, slipped inside, and closed it quietly behind me. I stepped in front of the mirror and looked at the purple-and-black aftermath of the beating. As I raised my head, I saw the imprints of my father's fingers on my neck. The pain of what he had tried to do almost overwhelmed me. And then I remembered . . . Jesus had laid His hand on my head. I remembered the tenderness, the love that had flowed through me. His words came rushing back. He loved me. Jesus loved me!

I wanted to tell someone, but I didn't dare. Mom would be horrified that I had given my life to Jesus. She told me if I ever became a Christian she would consider me dead and have a funeral for me. She said, "If you murder someone or become a drug addict or a homosexual, it would not give me as much heartbreak and grief as if you accepted Jesus." I'm not certain she actually meant it, but she did say it to me. Dad would think I was lying, and that always meant a beating. Instead, I held the events of the night inside and didn't tell anyone for years. Like Mary of old, I kept those things in my heart and thought of them often.

As the days wore on, I realized that Jesus had made other changes in my life that night. My speech impediment had instantly vanished. My stomach, which had always been prone to painful ulcer spasms, calmed and the pain stopped. My fears disappeared. No longer did I walk down the street with my eyes on my ragged sneakers. I was able to look people in the eye without fear.

Often I have wondered what my mom and dad thought about my miraculous deliverance from stuttering or the cessation of the stomach pain. Neither ever mentioned the change in me. Never wanting anyone to challenge my moment of hope, I kept my experience with Jesus and my salvation a secret.

I was convinced that I had to do something to earn God's love. I still saw God through the eyes of my father, and His love as being conditional. That was especially true since I had promised Him that when I turned twenty, I would tell the story to everyone. I had vowed, *"If you wait until I'm twenty, I will never take Your name in vain, and I'll never commit a sexual sin."*

I wish I could tell you that the abuse stopped at that very moment, but it didn't. The storms in our home raged on, but Christ had calmed me in their midst. The tumult would continue until I enlisted in the army at the age of sixteen and was inducted on July 1, the day after my seventeenth birthday.

That one brief sentence—*"Son, I love you and I have a wonderful plan for your life"*—revealed so very, very much to me. I was accepted. I was loved. I was not an accident or a blunder—the result of an adulterous affair. The awful things that had happened to me had not ruined me beyond repair. God had a plan—a wonderful plan—for my life. All I had to do was to follow His leading and He would direct me.

God's plan for your life is different from mine, but it is no less wonderful. You can rest assured that His perfect plan for your future includes neither barrenness nor bitterness. It is likely that my translation of this word from God was centered on my wanting to escape from the abuse that had been dished out for years. Perhaps I thought God would swoop down and zap my father the very next time Dad brought out the extension cord or coat hanger. I can tell you now that did not happen. Eventually, I grew in size to the point that the physical abuse stopped, but the verbal cruelty lasted much longer.

Verbal abuse undermines the parent/child bond and promotes the "labeling effect." Here, a child takes on the characteristics of the insulting and demeaning label used by the parent, such as "stupid, bastard, whore, troublemaker, lazy" and acts out that role. I was called "moron" so often by my father I actually began to believe I could not excel at anything; I was just garbage—a piece of valueless human trash that deserved to be discarded. I talked to and treated myself like trash. I took for granted that everyone else must have thought I was trash as well.

As victims, you and I may feel that we have every right to weep, to rail against the unfairness of it all. There are, however, Solomon's words from Ecclesiastes 3:1–4 (NIV):

> There is a time for everything, and a season for every activity under the heavens:
>
> a time to be born and a time to die,
> a time to plant and a time to uproot,
> a time to kill and a time to heal,
> a time to tear down and a time to build,
> a time to weep and a time to laugh,
> a time to mourn and a time to dance . . .

There is definitely a time for tears, but there comes a time when you and I must make the decision to move forward and retake lost ground. It is a time to blink back the tears and attack the flourishing outgrowth of symptoms, pain, and thorny problems produced by the abuse—a time to expose the root system and deal with its poisonous fruit. It is time to allow the Holy Spirit to bring His plow and break up the fallow ground of your life so that you do not sow the precious seed of your future among the choking weeds and painful thorns from your past.

My life was a miraculous testimony to God's grace and favor. The myriad ways that God has led and blessed me, my family, and my ministry is unbelievable, yet true. God led me to begin to work with the Jewish people. Like the apostle Paul who was driven into Arabia early in his ministry for a time of teaching and training, so God drew me aside from Massachusetts to South Korea. For fourteen months I spent my time in South Korea fulfilling my obligation to the U.S. Army and learning to pray on what is now called "Prayer Mountain."

Years later I discovered that after I returned home, Dr. Paul Cho purchased the mountain and made it a place of prayer. He said to me, "You are the first Christian to pray atop the mountain." He called me "Holy Ghost Kimchi Man, Seed of Abraham." I know now that God wanted me to learn to pray; learn to listen to Him; and learn how to seek His will and plan for my life. I knew a plan had been established for me; I just needed to know how to allow God to unlock His purpose in my life. Like Paul, I had to learn not to "kick against the goads" (Acts 26:14 NIV).

What does this mean? Dr. Charles Swindoll, author and former chancellor of Dallas Theological Institute, wrote of Christ's words to Paul during his encounter on the road to Damascus:

> Goads were typically made from slender pieces of timber, blunt on one end and pointed on the other. Farmers used the pointed end to urge a stubborn ox into motion. Occasionally,

the beast would kick at the goad. The more the ox kicked, the more likely the goad would stab into the flesh of its leg, causing greater pain.... Once you've seriously encountered Jesus, as Saul did, there's no escaping Him. His words and works follow you deep within your conscience.[43]

Jesus so often taught allegorically, through the use of parables. He painted word pictures based on the issues of the day. He taught of love, grace, mercy, compassion, forgiveness, and generosity. Jesus also answered with parables to counterpointed questions—the kind intended to test and/or humiliate this Teacher from Galilee. Luke wrote of such an encounter in chapter 10—the tale of the Good Samaritan. It began with Jesus having been questioned by a young expert in the law, one who taught or interpreted the Mosaic law. He issued a challenge:

"Teacher, what shall I do to inherit eternal life?"

Far from being stumped, Jesus responded in a way the questioner would certainly understand. He answered the question based on Scripture:

You shall love the Lord your God with all

your heart, with all your soul, and with all your strength. (Deuteronomy 6:5 NKJV)

Then Jesus added a phrase from Leviticus, "Love your neighbor as yourself" (Luke 10:27 NIV; Leviticus 19:18 NIV).

Perhaps the examiner asked out of curiosity to test Jesus' knowledge of the Torah; perhaps it was to contrast his own intellectual superiority compared to the simplicity of Jesus' teachings. Apparently the well-used ploy of answering a question with a question was practiced as early as the days of Christ, for the young man asked, "'And who is my neighbor?'" (Luke 10:29 NKJV). It may have been an attempt to shirk his responsibility, to sidestep the law, or at least to free himself from aiding anyone outside his own community or race. Let me assure you that the response did not catch Jesus by surprise; he was prepared with the illustration of the Good Samaritan:

> "A man was going down from Jerusalem to Jericho, when he was attacked by robbers. They stripped him of his clothes, beat him and went away, leaving him half dead. A priest happened to be going down the same road, and when he saw the man, he passed by on the other side. So too, a Levite, when he came

to the place and saw him, passed by on the other side. But a Samaritan, as he traveled, came where the man was; and when he saw him, he took pity on him. He went to him and bandaged his wounds, pouring on oil and wine. Then he put the man on his own donkey, brought him to an inn and took care of him. The next day he took out two denarii [the equivalent of two days' wages] and gave them to the innkeeper. 'Look after him,' he said, 'and when I return, I will reimburse you for any extra expense you may have.'" (Luke 10:30–35 NIV)

Jerusalem sat on a mountain ridge in Palestine 2,500 feet above sea level. Jericho, located on the Jordan River plain, was 853 feet below sea level. The seventeen-mile journey from the crest to the valley was a downward trek of over 3,300 feet through rocky ridges and desert places. There were sufficient places for robbers to hide and pounce on unsuspecting travelers, as they did to one sojourner. Not only was he robbed but also beaten, stripped of His clothing, and left for dead.

Then Jesus began to patiently explain to the young man

just who his neighbor was. He indicated that the first rubbernecker on the scene was a priest, soon followed by a Levite. Both represented the influential religious community. Because of their elevated positions in society, apparently each thought himself above stopping to give aid to one of a lower class. It may have been that both men pondered only long enough to ascertain that the wounded man was not a friend or neighbor—one from their own social strata. Maybe one or both could think of an appropriate passage from the Torah that would have prevented their ministering to the man.

God speaks to you and me so that we will treasure the truth, tread in the way of the truth, and transmit the truth to others along the way. Was my road of life pothole-free after I returned from South Korea? Not at all! I found myself living in a YMCA, robbed and left penniless, but that experience again drove me to my knees in search of God's plan. For a week in my sparsely furnished room, I shut myself in with God, fasting, praying, and searching the Scriptures, much as I had done in Korea. I had determined to drink only water as I beseeched God in prayer. I pointed to a battered chair in the corner and prayed, "Jesus, this is Your chair. If You want to come and talk with me I am ready to listen and obey. I want to hear Your voice again." Jesus' voice was silent. I determined to read through the entire New Testament as

I prayed. I was led to a Bible college in Texas, where I met my life partner, Carolyn, and we entered the ministry together. Smooth sailing, right? No, but years later I was led to contact Prime Minister Menachem Begin of Israel. When I knocked on that door and it was opened, it began what was, for me, my true life's work with the Jews in Israel. I have penned several books on the events in my life that have fueled and fed my desire to help my people. Ultimately, I was led to purchase and restore the Corrie ten Boom Holocaust Center in Haarlem, Holland. It had been Corrie's vision that it be restored. I flew to Haarlem by faith to follow God's leading. As I walked around the clock shop, I asked about seeing the upstairs where eight hundred Jews had been hidden during the Holocaust. The owner advised me that the door was kept locked, as it was only used for storage.

My heart broke. The Ten Boom clock shop should be open to the public as a testimony to the world of the love of a Christian family for the Jewish people. I prayed, "Lord, I want to buy this house and restore it. Help me." The next day I returned and asked the owner if he would sell the shop to me. Just as he refused my offer, the clocks in the shop began to toll the noon hour. He turned to me and asked, "Do you know what today is?" I mentioned the day of the week. "No," he said. "That is not what I meant—today is April 15, Corrie's birthday and the date of her death. And yes, I will sell the shop to you." I purchased the building and its contents, all of which became part of the restoration. In 2008, Casper and his daughter Betsie were honored at *Yad Vashem* as two of the Righteous Among the Nations. Corrie ten Boom had been honored in 1968. It was my great honor to have been invited to participate in the induction ceremony along with Israeli ambassador to the Netherlands Harry Kney-Tal.

I had no idea the purchase of the ten Boom home and clock shop would be the inspiration for the founding of the Jerusalem Prayer Team (JPT) in 2002 and later, the Friends of Zion Heritage Center and Museum. Today JPT, the largest prayer movement worldwide, has over twenty million members in over 100 countries.

JPT was based on a long-standing prayer meeting founded in 1844 by the ten Boom family patriarch. A weekly meeting to pray for the Jewish people followed a moving worship service in the Dutch Reformed Church of Reverend Witteveen. The first and second Great Awakenings that had swept Protestant Europe and North America played an important role in the yearning to pray for the Jewish people. Casper ten Boom felt the need to continue the weekly meetings, where the family and others who stopped by specifically prayed for the peace of Jerusalem (Psalm 122:6). These meetings took place for one hundred years, until February 28, 1944, when Nazi soldiers came to the house to take the family away for aiding local Jews. Following the tradition of the ten Boom family, the Jerusalem Prayer Team was founded to encourage people to continue to pray for the peace of Jerusalem and to help the Jewish people—God's chosen ones.

Just as God shaped the life of Paul, so He shaped *my* life according to His plan and purpose. I could readily relate to the abuse suffered by many who were targeted simply because they were Jewish. My own mother was often called a "Jew witch" when simply trying to buy groceries on the Fridays before Shabbat. She was the target of tomatoes and eggs simply because of her heritage. Because I could not defend her, I was determined to defend other Jewish people. God has made that possible.

It was the building of the Friends of Zion Museum that led to my close association with the late Shimon Peres, former Israeli prime minister and president. When the museum was near opening, I approached Mr. Peres and asked him to act as international chair for the organization; he readily agreed. We soon discovered that his rabbi grandfather and mine had belonged to that same synagogue in Belarus. The two men with the entire congregation had been herded into their place of worship, the doors nailed shut, and the building set afire. Every man, woman, and child inside was burned to death.

President Peres and I worked together to found the Friends of Zion Award, which was presented to former president George W. Bush and Prince Albert II of Monaco. We then traveled to Vatican City, where the award was given to Pope Francis. The former president of Israel told the pope about the fate of our grandfathers; Pope Francis and Shimon both wept as I shared my story. Peres' rabbi cantor grandfather was a teacher of the Talmud, but his hero was the chief rabbi of the synagogue—my great-grandfather Mikel Katznelson. After relating my story, the pope asked, "How did you, a Jew, come to Jesus Christ?" At that juncture, I was able to share how God had drawn me to Him and changed my life.

President Peres told the pope that he and I were family because of our shared experiences. Ten weeks later, Mr. Peres, Israel's ninth president, died and I was able to attend his funeral. Eighty-six world leaders were in attendance, including Queen Beatrice of the Netherlands, Prince Charles, former president George W. Bush, President Barack Obama, and former president Bill Clinton. I walked up to the VIP section and heard someone say as they pointed toward me, "He is family; let him through."

I believe the Friends of Zion Heritage Center is one more building block in the plan and purpose God has had for my life from the beginning of time. The Friends of Zion Heritage Center (FOZ), a $100-million project in Jerusalem, gained ten million members in its first year of operation. FOZ, just 600 meters from the temple mount, is ground zero for the global prayer movement. With over one billion Christian Zionists worldwide, the goal is to unite them to stand with Israel and the Jewish people. FOZ now has a vast social network platform to mobilize Israel's greatest friends. The organization already has more than one million members in Indonesia and is presently growing by a staggering two million members monthly. A massive communication hub there will be linked to the thousands of Christian television and radio outlets, as well as to churches and universities globally.

Just as Jesus knew me all those years ago, He knows you and has a great plan for your life. Is it too late to begin seeking His plan? Never!

Remember Joshua and Caleb? God promised to bring the children of Israel into a fertile land of blessing, a land filled with milk and honey. He encouraged them to be bold and to take it in His name. Numbers 13:2 says that when the people arrived at the border, God told them to send spies into the land to examine it.

After forty days, the spies returned from their mission carrying a cluster of grapes so big that *"they bare it between two upon a staff"* (v. 23). It was indeed a land of great wealth and promise!

Yet despite the bounty they saw in the land, eight of the ten men quaked with fear. God had not said anything about fighting giants! In Numbers 13:28 (KJV) we read:

> Nevertheless the people be strong that dwell in the land, and the cities are walled, and very great: and moreover we saw the children of Anak there.

An incredibly infectious fear gripped the hearts of the children of Israel. Joshua and Caleb stood up to the fearful spies and rebuked them for their unbelief. These two generals had not forgotten their days in slavery and were thankful to be delivered by a great and loving God. They knew they could take the land because of God's faithfulness. He had promised to fight their battles—even battles against giants.

Still, the people chose to believe a wicked report from the fearful majority rather than trust God's promise of success from a faith-filled minority. The people actually threatened to stone Joshua and Caleb—and incredibly begged Moses to allow them to return to Egyptian slavery! For their rebellion,

God made the children of Israel wander in the wilderness forty years until all the fearful, unbelieving people had died. Of that generation, men and women aged twenty and older, only Joshua and Caleb remained.

The Lord spared them because they demonstrated unyielding faith and obedience and were blessed for it; however, they also had to wander with the unbelieving masses in the desert. For forty years they put their dreams on hold. For forty years they waited for the promise to be fulfilled. And for forty years they continued to trust the Lord.

Unlike the rebellious children of Israel, the character of Joshua and Caleb was developed, their faith strengthened, and their obedience sharpened. When they walked from the wilderness across the Jordan River into the land of Canaan, Joshua and Caleb had become *mighty* men of valor for God.

Joshua was singled out to lead the people of Israel into the promised land after Moses died. Caleb was likewise blessed: Forty-five years after he and Joshua had spied out the land, at the age of eighty-five, Caleb was on the verge of inheriting God's promise to him.

Isn't it interesting that Caleb wanted to capture the same land he had seen in his younger days? The giants were still there, but they did not frighten him. He knew more than ever that God is a good God who is able and willing to deliver His people from the hand of the enemy.

Writer and editor John Greco wrote:

> Godly men and women had to trust God and stay close to Him. This meant seeking wisdom, talking with (and listening to) God in prayer, and looking to see where He was already at work in the world. It also meant obeying God's Word, even when doing so was costly. The faithful who have gone before us were no different than you or me. And the same keys to living life in step with God are available to us today.
>
> This kind of life is dangerous, though. It requires yielding to God, day in and day out. It requires giving up a check-the-boxes, seven-easy-steps-to-a-better-life approach to religion. It requires giving up control. *It requires a relationship.*[44]

No matter your age, no matter the stage of your life, you are never too old to follow God's plan and purpose for you. He will give you a new direction, a new plan, and renew your strength and capabilities to accomplish that which He has set forth for you to do.

SCRIPTURES ON GOD'S WILL

Matthew 6:10—Your will be done on earth as it is in heaven.

Matthew 7:21—Not everyone who says to me, "Lord, Lord," will enter the kingdom of heaven, but only he who does the will of my Father who is in heaven.

Ephesians 5:17—Therefore do not be foolish, but understand what the Lord's will is.

Hebrews 10:36—You need to persevere so that when you have done the will of God, you will receive what he has promised.

1 John 2:17—The world and its desires pass away, but the man who does the will of God lives forever.

Psalm 143:10—Teach me to do your will, for you are my God; may your good Spirit lead me on level ground.

Psalm 40:8—I desire to do your will, O my God; your law is within my heart.

Mark 3:33–35—Who are my mother and my brothers? he asked. Then he looked at those seated in a circle around him and said, Here are my mother and my brothers! Whoever does God's will is my brother and sister and mother.

Luke 22:42—Father, if you are willing, take this cup from me; yet not my will, but yours be done.

Hebrews 13:20–21—May the God of peace ... equip you with everything good for doing his will, and may he work in us what is pleasing to him, through Jesus Christ, to whom be glory for ever and ever. Amen.

16

"THE CONCLUSION OF MY FATHER'S STORY"

(SALVATION AND RESTORATION)

Mention the name Paul Harvey to the older generation and it's likely you will be rewarded with a nostalgic smile. Harvey was the 1950s, 1960s, and 1970s version of your favorite conservative commentator. According to Carlos Watson with National Public Radio, Harvey had a unique career sharing *The Rest of the Story* with his listeners:

> For more than three decades, from the 1970s to his death in 2009, Harvey would address his millions of listeners six days a week, giving them the backstory to people, things and events both famous and not-so-known.

From the origin of Coca-Cola to an account of JFK's assassination through his widow's eyes, from his tales of Elvis Presley's childhood to the Revolutionary War, the Oklahoma native had a magical fluidity to his storytelling. To hear him now is to feel at least a little nostalgic for that classic-radio mid-American accent—the kind that makes you think of political power in the 1940s and '50s, from FDR to Truman.[45]

In the pages of this book, I've shared some of my father's story. Now I want to tell you the rest of *his* story.

In James 5:16 (HCSB), the brother of Jesus gave us some disconcerting instructions:

> Therefore, confess your sins to one another and pray for one another, so that you may be healed. The urgent request of a righteous person is very powerful in its effect.

In Matthew 5:23–24 (NIV), Jesus taught:

> Therefore, if you are offering your gift at the altar and there remember that your brother or sister has something against you,

> leave your gift there in front of the altar. First go and be reconciled to them; then come and offer your gift.

In His teachings, Jesus pointed out that relationships take precedence over feelings, over sacrifices, over personal preferences. He said we are to confess our sins, to be reconciled to others. It is obvious that Jesus meant we are not to wait for the other person to make the first move; we are to take that first step. Jesus was not instituting a new law; He was stating a principle that we should follow, if possible. There are times when confessing a sin would badly hurt others, or when going to someone for reconciliation would be dangerous. Wise counsel from a pastor or counselor should be sought in those circumstances.

On one occasion I took my son, Michael, to see his grandfather. Dad wanted to show him his pride and joy—the fighting roosters he raised. As we walked toward them, Dad saw a cockerel lying on the ground. He stooped and picked it up and with great tenderness said, "Oh, that poor little thing. Its neck is broken." Then he looked up and said, "The dogs will eat it," and threw it over his shoulder. He turned to my son and said, "Michael, I'm an old man, and these roosters give me a reason to live." Michael shrugged and said with a hint of sarcasm, "Grandpa, that makes me feel really special."

Dad told me later that he dreamed repeatedly of trying to give me black stones. He said that in his dream the stones had been passed from his grandfather to his father, and I refused them because in my hand were white stones. It occurred to me that the black stones were representative of the generational curse that he was trying to pass along to me and his grandson. The white stones were symbolic of my life in Christ—a true commanded blessing.

Author and Bible teacher Beth Moore wrote of how to break generational curses:

> We must face generational strongholds head-on. If we don't, they can remain almost unrecognizable—but they don't remain benign. Family strongholds continue to be the seedbed for all sorts of destruction. Oftentimes we've grown up with these chains and they feel completely natural. We consider them part of our personality rather than a strangling yoke.
>
> Thankfully, Christians aren't doomed to live with our families' sins. The Cross of

> Calvary is enough to set us free from every yoke; God's Word is enough to make liberty a practical reality, no matter what those before us left as an "inheritance."[46]

In my later years, the Spirit of God began to impress me that I needed to apologize to my dad. Why? He had never shown any remorse for his treatment of me and my siblings; why should I be the one to say "I'm sorry" to him? I wrestled with that for some time. I pondered the questions: What does God have in mind? What could possibly be accomplished by my humbling myself to ask forgiveness of the man who so brutally abused me? I finally acquiesced to that still, small voice, the one that has guided me since the age of eleven.

One morning I awoke and asked Carolyn to purchase the airline tickets that would take me to Alabama and my father's home. Talk about a step of faith! I had no idea what to expect. As I boarded the flight later that week, I prayed for God's direction and for Him to put His words in my mouth and not my own.

From Atlanta, Georgia, I drove the back roads that would take me to Dad's mobile home outside Dothan, Alabama. Parking the rental car in his yard, I made my way to the steps that led to the kitchen. Dad was visible through the window in the door and was dozing in his recliner in the living room. I eased the door open and stepped inside. The odors of mildew, stale beer, and scorched food were overwhelming. I eyed the kitchen counter, which was a sea of half-empty prescription bottles.

Gently I called, "Dad, it's me. Michael." He roused from his nap, and as I stepped closer, I could see that his clothes were stained with food and his hair was lank and dirty. How long had it been since he had showered? Seeing me in the kitchen, Dad righted his recliner, reached for the television remote, muted the sound, and stood. He walked unsteadily toward me. "What are you doing here?" he growled. "Don't you have places to be and important people to see?"

"I came to see you, Dad. I have something very important to discuss with you. Why don't we sit down in the living room so we can talk?"

We moved to the living room and I sat on the edge of the sofa while Dad lowered himself back into his favorite chair. As soon as he was settled, I slid forward and knelt on the floor beside him. He snarled and asked sarcastically, "Just what do you think you're doing?" For an instant I was back in the house at 77 Pasco Road, groveling beside the chair in the living room, begging my father not to hit me again.

Just as quickly, I pushed that image from my mind. I reached out tentatively and laid my hand on Dad's arm and looked him squarely in his bloodshot eyes. "Dad, I want to ask you to forgive me." At the sound of those words, something leapt inside of me; it was as if from deep down in my spirit, a fresh, light breeze began to blow through my soul.

Dad's mouth literally dropped open. "Huh?" His eyebrows wrinkled in a frown. "Forgive you for what?" He punched a button on the remote and turned off the television.

I took a deep breath and exhaled before answering him: "Forgive me for disrespecting you. The Bible says we're supposed to honor our parents, but I never honored or respected you. It was wrong for me to carry that inside all this time. Will you forgive me?"

We sat there, staring at each other for what seemed like an eternity. Then Dad's face crumpled and tears seeped out of the corners of his eyes. "You're apologizing to me, and I'm the one who committed the unpardonable sin for what I did to you," he stammered. Shocked, I pondered his statement for a moment as I whispered a prayer for guidance. Quickly, perfect words flowed freely. "No, Dad. God loves you, and so do I. And this time, I really mean it."

Dad looked shocked. "How can you say that after everything I've done? Back when I talked to God, I asked Him to forgive me a thousand times. I never thought He would, and I never thought none of my kids would ever want to have anything to do with me."

I assured Dad that he was forgiven, only to find him reaching toward me. It was all I could do not to flinch from his touch as his fingers brushed the top of my head. I asked him to pray for me. He was certain that God didn't want to hear from him, but I persuaded him otherwise. As I knelt by his chair, Dad began to pray and then sob out a prayer that began with him asking God to forgive me, but soon turned to him asking for God's forgiveness. After a few minutes, Dad leaned back in his recliner, wiped his eyes and nose on the bottom of his shirt, and then threw his arms around my shoulders. As stunned as I was, I managed to gather his large body in my arms.

After a few minutes, he disengaged and said, "The last time I cried like that was when I buried my mother." We visited for a while longer, then I arose; I had to get back to the airport in Charlotte. Dad looked up and said haltingly, "You have no idea what this means to me, Michael, you having come like this." He struggled up from his chair and walked with me to the door.

"Will you come back to see me?" he asked.

"Yes, Dad, I'll be back. And Dad? I love you."

That was the most freeing trip of my entire life.

God's grace and mercy captivated me. I found my heart overflowing with compassion for the man I thought I could never forgive, much less love, and I led him to Christ there in his living room. That was the beginning of a healing process that lasted until the day he died. As a young man, I had paid my father's house and car payments without any thanks from him. In the last weeks of Dad's life, he willed all of his belongings to me—everything he owned. I spoke at his funeral and talked about his late conversion to Christ, his record as a war hero, and how much he loved his mother. Sadly, those were the only good things I could say about him.

I am overjoyed to say that God's favor on my life has been so bounteous that I was in turn able to give my father's entire estate to my six siblings.

Healing in my own life has been a work in progress and, with God's help, I have learned not to listen to the lies of the Enemy of my soul. Rather than listen to the old negative talk, I have replaced it with what God's Word says about me as His child. I have learned at His feet that what God values is not what my pride or my compulsive workaholic traits can accomplish—it is me: Mike Evans, His child.

Forgiveness! What a freeing act of the will. With Jesus' teachings on love, grace, and forgiveness, He turned the old "eye for an eye" crowd on its collective head. His thanks for freeing them from that life of revenge was an arrest, a kangaroo-court conviction, a beating, mockery, and crucifixion. He had been marched through the streets of Jerusalem struggling to drag the cross of torture on His shoulders. Then He had collapsed on Golgotha, the hill of execution. The spikes and ropes were in place and the cross was raised against the sky. With a thud, it hurtled unimpeded into the hole that would hold it upright.

Some in the crowd looked upon Jesus—naked before the world, beaten to within an inch of His life, bruised and bloody—with satisfaction. I can easily imagine that Satan and all the demons in hell were dancing with glee. Their purpose had been accomplished. The Son of God was near death. The Enemy was certain he had won. Other bystanders bowed their heads in shame and compassion. Their beloved friend and companion hung exposed to the world. Tears rolled down those faces, and sobs could be heard echoing from the hill. As they watched in agony, the indifferent soldiers gathered in a circle at the foot of the cross. "Where are the dice?" one called. "Let's cast lots for His clothes."

As they began to gamble, a whisper issued from the mouth of Jesus and echoed through the halls of eternity.

His first words spoken from the cross were "Father, forgive them, for they do not know what they are doing" (Luke 23:34 NIV).

Astonished, the soldiers must have momentarily halted their grisly game and looked heavenward. They were accustomed to hearing screams and curses, pleas of innocence, entreaties for mercy, appeals for water, but a prayer for forgiveness? Unimaginable!

The Man on the cross had prayed for them, pleading for God's forgiveness for their actions! The Son knew the Father in all of His mercy and His richly abounding love. He knew the words penned in Exodus:

> "The Lord, the Lord, the compassionate and gracious God, slow to anger, abounding in love and faithfulness, maintaining love to thousands, and forgiving wickedness, rebellion and sin." (Exodus 34:6–7 NIV)

Did those men even know the name of the Man they had nailed to the cross—whose side they would pierce? Did they know His name was Jesus and that He was the Lamb of God, the One whom God had loved before the foundations of the world were even laid? It is likely none knew just how much they would need the forgiveness offered by the

One hanging above them. They simply heard His words of petition to the Father.

None understood that Jesus had taken on the role of advocate, defending the actions of those who had wronged Him. His teachings of "Love your enemies, bless those who curse you, do good to those who hate you, and pray for those who spitefully use you and persecute you" (Matthew 5:44 NKJV) were more than mere utterances; they were a lifestyle. It was an act of the will. He was teaching a world what true forgiveness really is.

Jesus taught that there was a relationship between forgiving and receiving God's forgiveness:

> "And whenever you stand praying, if you have anything against anyone, forgive him, that your Father in heaven may also forgive you your trespasses. But if you do not forgive, neither will your Father in heaven forgive your trespasses." (Mark 11:25–26 NKJV)

The prayer for forgiveness on the cross was not meant to be the last act of a dying man; it was an example for His followers. As they had been forgiven, so were they to forgive those who sinned against them (see Matthew 6:9–13, the Lord's Prayer). Of course, it is often more readily talked about than practiced. It takes tremendous courage to exercise that kind of forgiveness. But it will bring you favor with God and the freedom to be healed emotionally and physically.

In Colossians 2:13–15 (NKJV), Paul wrote:

> And you, being dead in your trespasses and the uncircumcision of your flesh, He has made alive together with Him, having forgiven you all trespasses, having wiped out the handwriting of requirements that was against us, which was contrary to us. And He has taken it out of the way, having nailed it to the cross. Having disarmed principalities and powers, He made a public spectacle of them, triumphing over them in it.

Evangelist and teacher Oswald Chambers wrote of forgiveness:

> Forgiveness is the divine miracle of grace. The cost to God was the Cross of Christ. To forgive sin, while remaining a holy God, this price had to be paid. Never accept a view of the fatherhood of God if it blots out the atonement. The revealed truth of God is that

without the atonement He cannot forgive—He would contradict His nature if He did. The only way we can be forgiven is by being brought back to God through the atonement of the Cross. God's forgiveness is possible only in the supernatural realm.

Compared with the miracle of the forgiveness of sin, the experience of sanctification is small. Sanctification is simply the wonderful expression or evidence of the forgiveness of sins in a human life. But the thing that awakens the deepest fountain of gratitude in a human being is that God has forgiven his sin. Paul never got away from this. Once you realize all that it cost God to forgive you, you will be held as in a vise, constrained by the love of God.[48]

Forgiveness is a matter of life and death for the forgiven. It was a fall evening in Jerusalem at the conclusion of the Feast of Tabernacles. Jesus had spent the night on the Mount of Olives and had risen early to make His way to the temple to connect with people gathering there in the dawn's light. Suddenly He heard a commotion—men shouting, the sound punctuated by the screams of a woman being manhandled up the rocky stairs and into the courtyard. She was exhausted from struggling to free herself from her captors. Tears stained her face, and her scanty clothing was dirty and bedraggled. Sheer terror distorted her features as she realized she was about to die at the hands of an angry mob.

The target of the scribes and Pharisees was sitting beneath the portico preparing to teach. Reaching Jesus, they hurled the woman down at His feet. As she cowered on the ground, the pain of her skinned hands and knees was nothing compared to the sentence that would be passed on her. Jesus made no overt move toward her or the men.

The charges brought by those hypocrites—and their purpose—are outlined in John 8:4–6 (NKJV):

> "Teacher, this woman was caught in adultery, in the very act. Now Moses, in the law, commanded us that such should be stoned. But what do You say?" This they said, testing Him, that they might have something of which to accuse Him.

Oh, how respectful were the self-righteous to the man they were trying to trick; they called Him "Teacher." But how little they really knew about what He taught. The adultery charge could only be levied against the woman if she were married or betrothed, which was tantamount to marriage in those times. Since the Mosaic Law required that a married adulterer be strangled, it was highly likely that this was a young woman engaged to be married. She was utterly humiliated as she lay on the ground before the crowd and her adversaries. I wonder if she knew the Man before whom they had dragged her. Did she know she was about to be judged by grace and forgiveness personified in the Lamb of God?

Were the men surprised that Jesus failed to react to their accusations? The Bible does not reveal how many times they asked Him the same question: "What do you say?" Surely at His silence her challengers began to grow frustrated with the calm and methodical Jesus. As their words whirled around Him, Jesus leaned over and began to write on the ground. We are not told what He wrote, only that He did.

Finally the Righteous Judge began to speak words that must have chilled the hearts of those gathered:

> "He who is without sin among you, let him throw a stone at her first." And again He stooped down and wrote on the ground. (vv. 7–8 NKJV)

Now, the law of Moses required that in order for a sentence to be carried out, there had to be two witnesses to bring the charges. Had the angry mob thought through the ramifications of the charges against the young woman? It would be their duty to pick up stones and take the life of the person on the ground before them. The men who had plotted against this woman in order to trap Jesus had likely not counted the entire cost of their actions. Were they cold-hearted and brutal enough to carry out their own sentence against her? They were suddenly caught off-guard. Now the proverbial ball was in their court.

Perhaps to give them time to think about the consequences of their actions, Jesus again leaned over and wrote on the ground:

> Then those who heard it, being convicted by their conscience, went out one by one, beginning with the oldest even to the last. And Jesus was left alone, and the woman standing in the midst. (v. 9 NKJV)

One by one the men began to slink away into the shadows. As the noise abated, the woman began to realize that something was happening. Raising her head slightly, she peeked around only to see that she was left alone with this Teacher, the one they called Jesus:

> When Jesus had raised Himself up and saw no one but the woman, He said to her, "Woman, where are those accusers of yours? Has no one condemned you?" She said, "No one, Lord." And Jesus said to her, "Neither do I condemn you; go and sin no more." (vv. 10–11 NKJV)

Was it at that moment she understood—forgiveness was hers for the asking? She saw only kindness and peace in the eyes of the Man before her—not the disgust she had witnessed from her accusers earlier. She was still guilty of adultery, still worthy of death; now what would happen to her? Not one of her accusers was left to demand judgment. And in the whirl of controversy, she offered no justification for her sin, no declaration of her innocence, no defense of her actions. She stood totally exposed. And yet the One standing before her offered freedom from condemnation, but He required one thing from her—a repudiation of her sinful lifestyle.

The Mosaic law could offer only condemnation and retaliation. She needed the same thing her accusers needed: forgiveness of sin and abundant grace. At no time did Jesus belittle this young woman for her immorality; not once did He shout angrily at her. He offered only hope and renewal; Jesus provided exactly what she was lacking—life and peace, grace and forgiveness.

Under the law, the sacrifice of perfect, unblemished lambs was required to assuage God's anger and postpone His judgment. It was the Person of Jesus Christ, the sinless Lamb of God who offered His life on the cross. He became the once-for-all-time sacrifice for sin so that you and I could be reconciled with the Father.

SCRIPTURES ON RESTORATION

Joel 2:25–26—And I will restore to you the years that the locust hath eaten, the cankerworm, and the caterpiller, and the palmerworm, my great army which I sent among you.

Jeremiah 30:17—For I will restore health unto thee, and I will heal thee of thy wounds, saith the Lord; because they called thee an Outcast, saying, This is Zion, whom no man seeketh after.

Psalm 51:12—Restore unto me the joy of thy salvation; and uphold me with thy free spirit.

Isaiah 61:7—For your shame ye shall have double; and for confusion they shall rejoice in their portion: therefore in their land they shall possess the double: everlasting joy shall be unto them.

Job 42:10—And the Lord turned the captivity of Job, when he prayed for his friends: also the Lord gave Job twice as much as he had before.

1 John 5:4—For whatsoever is born of God overcometh the world: and this is the victory that overcometh the world, even our faith.

Mark 11:24—Therefore I say unto you, What things soever ye desire, when ye pray, believe that ye receive them, and ye shall have them.

1 Peter 5:10—But the God of all grace, who hath called us unto his eternal glory by Christ Jesus, after that ye have suffered a while, make you perfect, stablish, strengthen, settle you.

Zechariah 9:12—Turn you to the strong hold, ye prisoners of hope: even to day do I declare that I will render double unto thee;

Jeremiah 29:11—For I know the thoughts that I think toward you, saith the Lord, thoughts of peace, and not of evil, to give you an expected end.

Galatians 6:1—Brethren, if a man be overtaken in a fault, ye which are spiritual, restore such an one in the spirit of meekness; considering thyself, lest thou also be tempted.

17

FORGIVENESS

(A DECISION OF THE WILL)

Forgiveness and reconciliation can be a thorny issue. Often, hearts are hard and unreceptive. Feelings have been flayed, salt poured into the wounds, and emotions are raw. The one offended may not even want to be in the same room with the offender, much less hear what he or she may have to say.

Only God can heal a wounded heart and broken relationships. The one exercise that can bring resolution is prayer. I'm sure you've heard it said that prayer changes things. It not only changes *things*, it changes people.

Corrie ten Boom is well-known for her role in aiding Jews in escaping from the Netherlands during the Holocaust. She and her sister, Betsie, were arrested and eventually incarcerated in Ravensbrück, a Nazi death camp.

In October 1972, I held a series of meetings in Texarkana, a town located on the Texas–Arkansas border. The drive over from Fort Worth was too far to go back and forth each day so I stayed at the Texarkana Holiday Inn. One afternoon as I came from the parking lot I noticed an elderly lady who was headed toward the entrance to the hotel lobby. She was carrying a suitcase, and the thought came to me that I should help her. I stepped quickly to her side and reached to open the door. "May I carry your bag for you?" I asked.

"Thank you," she replied, "but there's no need. I am but a tramp for the Lord." She spoke with a heavy European accent and when she smiled her face lit up.

That's when I realized who she was. "Corrie ten Boom!" I exclaimed like a star-struck kid. "I've read your book *The Hiding Place*. I never imagined I would get to meet you. And certainly not here."

She smiled and clasped my hand. "You can carry my suitcase if you'll join me for a cup of soup."

"I would love to," I replied.

Corrie checked in at the front desk, and then we walked together to the hotel restaurant. As we enjoyed our soup together, she shared with me her great love for the Jewish people.

Faced with Nazi atrocities, the Ten Booms began rescuing their Jewish neighbors, secreting them away in a hiding place inside their home and in locations throughout the countryside. When the Nazis learned of the prayer meetings and of the Ten Boom family's work in rescuing Jews, Corrie, her father, and sister were arrested and sent to Ravensbrück, a concentration camp.

When she paused to take a spoonful of soup, I asked, "Who is your favorite Bible character?"

"King David, and my favorite of his psalms is the ninety-first. God gave me that psalm on my birthday, while I was in Ravensbrück.

"It was April 15, and I said, 'Lord, this is my birthday. I would like a birthday present.' He whispered, *'Your present is Psalm 91.'*"

Then she quoted the first verse. "'Whoever dwells in the shelter of the Most High will rest in the shadow of the Almighty.'" She explained, "Living in that shelter—*that hiding place*—means living before an audience of one and seeking Christ's affirmation above that of the world."

As we parted, she reminded, "You must remember what Jesus said: 'You will seek me and find me when you seek me with all of your heart'" (Jeremiah 29:13 NIV).

I didn't know it then but that chance meeting with Miss ten Boom was the start of a lifelong association with her story and her work.

Her sister, Betsie, did not survive the horrors of her captivity, but Corrie was eventually released due incredibly to a clerical error. After a time, the story of her wartime experiences began to reach other countries. She was invited to speak in America, England, and many other nations. The most difficult place for her to visit was Germany, a land scarred by bombs and hatred. Its cities were heaps of rubble, the citizens' minds and hearts covered with the ashes of despair. Corrie knew that the Lord would "give them beauty for ashes, the oil of joy for mourning, [and] the garment of praise for the spirit of heaviness" (see Isaiah 61:3 NKJV) if only the German citizens would surrender their lives to the living Lord.

In Corrie's own words, she described an encounter with one of the former guards from Ravensbrück. It was one of the guards who had patrolled the showers where she and Betsie were forced to strip naked upon entry to the camp:

> At a church service in Munich I saw the former SS man who had stood guard outside

the shower room . . . He came up to me and said, "How grateful I am for your message, Fraulein. To think that He has washed my sins away!" He thrust his hand out to shake mine . . . I who had so often preached the need to forgive kept my hand at my side . . . I breathed a silent prayer: Jesus, I cannot forgive him. Give me Your forgiveness. As I took his hand the most incredible thing happened . . . a current seemed to pass from me to him, while into my heart sprang a love for this stranger that almost overwhelmed me.[45]

Forgiveness means bestowing freedom instead of the punishment I feel my abuser deserves. Forgiveness means giving love and understanding when the enemy expects only hatred and revenge. Forgiveness means turning over to God my desires to blame, defame, and punish my offender.

I cannot be released from my offender or from the anger-arousing, shame-evoking, esteem-shattering memories connected with his/her offenses against me until I accept wholeheartedly God's way of forgiveness. Forgiveness is a releasing, transforming experience.

You and I cannot be transformed or truly separated from the past until we accept God's way of forgiveness. But what is God's way? The apostle Paul, whose body was crisscrossed with scars from bloody beatings, who understood from firsthand experience what it was to be homeless, hungry, thirsty, and unjustly imprisoned, exhorted:

> Bless those who persecute you [who are cruel in their attitude toward you]; bless and do not curse them. Repay no one evil for evil, but take thought for what is honest and proper and noble [aiming to be above reproach] in the sight of everyone. If possible, as far as it depends on you, live at peace with everyone. Beloved, never avenge yourselves, but leave the way open for [God's] wrath; for it is written, Vengeance is Mine, I will repay (requite), says the Lord. Do not let yourself be overcome by evil, but overcome (master) evil with good. (Romans 12:14, 17–19, 21 AMPC)

What was Paul's motivation for forgiving? It was the example of Jesus Christ, who bore the penalty for our sins (see Colossians 2:14). Therefore, "Be ye kind one to another," Paul pleads, "tenderhearted, forgiving one another, even as God for Christ's sake hath forgiven you" (Ephesians 4:32 KJV).

Forgiveness is not an emotion; it is an act of the will. Because if, even after having chosen to forgive someone, we still feel anger or pain, we mistakenly assume we have not forgiven.

If, after I choose to forgive, I do not feel as if I have forgiven, I must continue to keep my will set on obeying God. I must allow myself all the time and effort it takes to work through the stages of pain, misery, or sorrow. Anger, for example, must be acknowledged and dealt with or someday it will surface in full force and deal with me. It is a daily choice for you and me to believe His Word and receive His grace and peace. Eventually our emotions will fall into line with the decision to forgive.

God's plan for your life is different from mine, but it is no less wonderful. You can rest assured that His perfect plan for your future includes neither barrenness nor bitterness.

That is why you cannot find true release from your past or realize lasting personal growth and fulfillment by following formulas and rules. You need firm faith and a real relationship with the Lord Jesus Christ.

The writer of Psalm 126 must have known much about broken and painful relationships, for he wrote:

> They who sow in tears shall reap in joy. He who continually goes forth weeping, bearing seed for sowing, shall doubtless come again with rejoicing, bringing his sheaves *with him*. (Psalm 126:5–6 NKJV)

It is time to allow the Holy Spirit to bring His plow and break up the fallow ground of your life so that you do not sow the precious seed of your future among the choking weeks and painful thorns from your past.

Your future is bright because God's promises have not changed. When you need salvation, deliverance, healing, forgiveness, or restoration, go to Jesus. He is the Bread of Life, the Living Water, the Lion of Judah, the Rock of Ages, and the King of Kings!

SCRIPTURES ON FORGIVENESS

Mark 11:25—And when ye stand praying, forgive, if ye have ought against any: that your Father also which is in heaven may forgive you your trespasses.

Ephesians 4:32—And be ye kind one to another, tenderhearted, forgiving one another, even as God for Christ's sake hath forgiven you.

Matthew 6:15—But if ye forgive not men their trespasses, neither will your Father forgive your trespasses.

1 John 1:9—If we confess our sins, he is faithful and just to forgive us our sins, and to cleanse us from all unrighteousness.

Luke 6:27—But I say unto you which hear, Love your enemies, do good to them which hate you,

Luke 6:37—Judge not, and ye shall not be judged: condemn not, and ye shall not be condemned: forgive, and ye shall be forgiven:

Colossians 3:13—Forbearing one another, and forgiving one another, if any man have a quarrel against any: even as Christ forgave you, so also do ye.

1 Corinthians 10:13—There hath no temptation taken you but such as is common to man: but God is faithful, who will not suffer you to be tempted above that ye are able; but will with the temptation also make a way to escape, that ye may be able to bear it.

ENDNOTES

1. In the 1940s, military personnel were given "goofballs" during WWII in the South Pacific region to allow soldiers to tolerate the heat and humidity of daily working conditions. Goofballs were distributed to lower the respiratory system and blood pressure to combat the extreme conditions. Many soldiers returned with addictions that required several months of rehabilitation before discharge. http://en.wikipedia.org/wiki/Barbiturate; accessed November 2011.

2. https://womenmentoringwomen.me/2012/03/24/7-things-that-can-hinder-you-from-achieving-your-goals/; accessed January 2017.

3. "Death by a Thousand Cuts," Times Higher Education, May 8, 2008, https://www.timeshighereducation.com/books/death-by-a-thousand-cuts/401789.article; accessed January 2017.

4. Whitney Hopler, "Overcome Insecurity," Taken from: Robin Weidner's book, *Secure in Heart: Overcoming Insecurity in a Woman's Life* (Discipleship Publications International, 2007); http://www.crosswalk.com/faith/women/overcome-insecurity-11570022.html; accessed March 2017.

5. Originally from *Our Daily Bread*, the original concept for this story is found online at: http://www.christianglobe.com/Illustrations/theDetails.asp?whichOne=p&whichFile=protection.

6. Rev. Dr. Allen Hunt, "God's Promises for You: I Will Never Leave You nor Forsake You," http://day1.org/1027-gods_promises_for_you_i_will_never_leave_you_nor_forsake_you; accessed January 2016.

7. Rev. Paul Aiello, Jr., http://www.sermonsearch.com/sermon-illustrations/3911/lighthouse/; accessed November 2014.

8. Rev. David Albert Farmer, "Potiphar's Wife's Lies," http://sermonsfromsilverside.blogspot.com/2011/03/potiphars-wifes-lies.html; accessed March 2017.

9. Vance Havner, http://www.goodreads.com/quotes/97169-god-uses-broken-things-it-takes-broken-soil-to-produce; accessed December 2014.

10. "What does it mean that God speaks in a still small voice?" Got Questions Ministries, https://www.gotquestions.org/still-small-voice.html; accessed January 2017.

11. Dietrich Bonhoeffer, *Life Together* (New York: Harper and Row Publishers, 1954), 79.

12. Julie Boehlke, "The Effects of Parents Teasing Their Child," July 2011, http://www.livestrong.com/article/489418-the-effects-of-parents-teasing-their-child/; accessed February 2017.

13. Mark Hall, Casting Crowns—Does Anybody Hear Her Lyrics | MetroLyrics, http://www.metrolyrics.com/does-anybody-hear-her-lyrics-casting-crowns.html; accessed December 2014.

14. http://thinkexist.com/quotations/lies/; accessed February 2017.

15. Paul Lee Tan, *Encyclopedia of 7,700 Illustrations* (Rockville, MD: Assurance Publishers, 1988), p. 459 (1776).

16. Dr. Jeremy Myers, "Luke 6:27—Loving Those You'd Rather Hate," https://redeeminggod.com/sermons/luke/luke_6_27/; accessed February 2017.

17. Dr. Ralph Wilson, "18: Love Your Enemies," http://www.jesuswalk.com/lessons/6_27-36.htm; accessed February 2017.

18. Oswald Chambers, "The Purpose of Prayer," https://utmost.org/the-purpose-of-prayer/; accessed February 2017.

19. C.S. Lewis quote, https://sites.google.com/site/sayingquotes/cs-lewis; accessed March 2017.

20. http://www.actsweb.org/articles/article.php?i=1247&d=2&c=6; accessed February 2017.

21. http://thinkexist.com/quotation/there_are_two_great_days_in_a_person-s_life-the/331059.html; accessed February 2017.

22. C. H. Spurgeon, "The Obedience of Faith," August 2, 1890, at the Metropolitan Tabernacle, Newington.

23. Hudson Taylor Quotes: http://christian-quotes.ochristian.com/Hudson-Taylor-Quotes/; accessed September 2012.

24. https://bible.org/illustration/he-brought-me-here; accessed February 2017.

25. C. H. Spurgeon, "My times are in thy hand," https://www.blueletterbible.org/Comm/spurgeon_charles/sermons/2205.cfm; accessed February 2017.

26. https://www.brainyquote.com/quotes/quotes/w/washington149294.html; accessed February 2017.

27. Tara Lemieux, "I Just Helped Him to Cry," http://mindfullymusing.com/2013/08/27/i-just-helped-him-to-cry/; accessed February 2017.

28. Mark Stephenson, "You Are God's Child," https://today.reframemedia.com/devotionals/you-are-gods-child-2008-08-25; Accessed February 2017.

29. Ray Stedman, "God is Light," http://www.raystedman.org/new-testament/1-john/god-is-light; accessed February 2017.

30. Joel Pankow, "God's Light Shines in the Darkness," http://www.sermoncentral.com/sermons/gods-light-shines-in-the-darkness-joel-pankow-sermon-on-forgiveness-in-jesus-163572?page=6; accessed February 2017.

31. Paul Lee Tan, *Encyclopedia of 7,700 Illustrations* (Rockville, MD: Assurance Publishers, 1988), p. 459 (5824).

32. Holly Starr, "Through My Father's Eyes," Holly Starr Publishing (SESAC), Plight Music Publishing (SESAC), My Friend Cabo Music (SESAC); http://life1019.com/songs/through-my-fathers-eyes/; accessed March 2017.

33. "He Washed My Eyes With Tears," http://www.namethathymn.com/hymn-lyrics-detective-forum/index.php?a=vtopic&t=157; accessed February 2017.

34. Charles A. Miles, "In the Garden," http://library.timelesstruths.org/music/In_the_Garden/; accessed March 2017.

35. "Noah Found Grace in the Eyes of the Lord," http://artists.letssingit.com/statler-brothers-lyrics-noah-found-grace-in-the-eyes-of-the-lord-sv36796#ixzz1zCNJs7Nv; accessed June 2012.

36. C. H. Spurgeon, "The Obedience of Faith," August 2, 1890, at the Metropolitan Tabernacle, Newington.

37. Kurt Kaiser, "O How He Loves You and Me," http://www.angelfire.com/nf/music4christ/k-s/ohowhelyrics.html; accessed March 2017.

38. Susan Forward and Joan Torres, *Men Who Hate Women and the Women Who Love Them* (New York: Bantam Books, 1986) 144–145.

39. Jeff VanVonderen, *Good News for the Chemically Dependent* (Nashville: Thomas Nelson Publishers, 1984), 78–80.

40. Edward Mote, "My Hope Is Built on Nothing Less," https://en.wikipedia.org/wiki/My_Hope_Is_Built_on_Nothing_Less; accessed March 2017.

41. https://en.wikipedia.org/wiki/Agape; accessed March 2017.

42. Max Lucado, *Grace for the Moment* (Nashville, TN: J. Countryman, a division of Thomas Nelson, Inc., 2000), 29.

43. Dr. Charles Swindoll, "How Did Paul 'Kick Against the Goads'?" http://www.jesus.org/early-church-history/the-apostle-paul/how-did-paul-kick-against-the-goads.html

44. John Greco, "God's Perfect Plan for Your Life," http://www.boundless.org/faith/2013/gods-perfect-plan-for-your-life; accessed March 2017.

45. Carlos Watson, "The Rest of the Story: Paul Harvey, Conservative Talk Radio Pioneer," http://www.npr.org/2014/10/09/354718833/the-rest-of-the-story-paul-harvey-conservative-talk-radio-pioneer

46. Beth Moore, "Is there a 'generational curse' for sin?" *Today's Christian Woman*, May 2004, http://www.todayschristianwoman.com/articles/2004/may/beth-moore-breaking-free-generational-curse-sin.html; accessed March 2017.

47. Earl Jabay, *The Kingdom of Self*, Logos International, 1980.

48. Oswald Chambers, *My Utmost for His Highest*, "The Forgiveness of God," http://utmost.org/the-forgiveness-of-god/; accessed September 2014.

MICHAEL DAVID EVANS, the #1 *New York Times* bestselling author, is an award-winning journalist/Middle East analyst. Dr. Evans has appeared on hundreds of network television and radio shows including *Good Morning America, Crossfire* and *Nightline*, and *The Rush Limbaugh Show*, and on Fox Network, *CNN World News*, NBC, ABC, and CBS. His articles have been published in the *Wall Street Journal, USA Today, Washington Times, Jerusalem Post* and newspapers worldwide. More than twenty-five million copies of his books are in print, and he is the award-winning producer of nine documentaries based on his books.

Dr. Evans is considered one of the world's leading experts on Israel and the Middle East, and is one of the most sought-after speakers on that subject. He is the chairman of the board of the ten Boom Holocaust Museum in Haarlem, Holland, and is the founder of Israel's first Christian museum located in the Friends of Zion Heritage Center in Jerusalem.

Dr. Evans has authored a number of books including: *History of Christian Zionism, Showdown with Nuclear Iran, Atomic Iran, The Next Move Beyond Iraq, The Final Move Beyond Iraq,* and *Countdown.* His body of work also includes the novels *Seven Days, GameChanger, The Samson Option, The Four Horsemen, The Locket, Born Again: 1967,* and *The Columbus Code.*

✦ ✦ ✦

Michael David Evans is available to speak or for interviews.
Contact: EVENTS@drmichaeldevans.com.

BOOKS BY: MIKE EVANS

Israel: America's Key to Survival
Save Jerusalem
The Return
Jerusalem D.C.
Purity and Peace of Mind
Who Cries for the Hurting?
Living Fear Free
I Shall Not Want
Let My People Go
Jerusalem Betrayed
Seven Years of Shaking: A Vision
The Nuclear Bomb of Islam
Jerusalem Prophecies
Pray For Peace of Jerusalem
America's War: The Beginning of the End
The Jerusalem Scroll
The Prayer of David
The Unanswered Prayers of Jesus
God Wrestling
The American Prophecies
Beyond Iraq: The Next Move
The Final Move beyond Iraq
Showdown with Nuclear Iran
Jimmy Carter: The Liberal Left and World Chaos
Atomic Iran
Cursed
Betrayed
The Light
Corrie's Reflections & Meditations
The Revolution
The Final Generation
Seven Days
The Locket
Persia: The Final Jihad

GAMECHANGER SERIES:
GameChanger
Samson Option
The Four Horsemen

THE PROTOCOLS SERIES:
The Protocols
The Candidate

Jerusalem
The History of Christian Zionism
Countdown
Ten Boom: Betsie, Promise of God
Commanded Blessing
Born Again: 1948
Born Again: 1967
Presidents in Prophecy
Stand with Israel
Prayer, Power and Purpose
Turning Your Pain Into Gain
Christopher Columbus, Secret Jew
Living in the F.O.G.
Finding Favor with God
Finding Favor with Man
Unleashing God's Favor
The Jewish State: The Volunteers
See You in New York
Friends of Zion: Patterson & Wingate
The Columbus Code
The Temple
Satan, You Can't Have My Country!
Satan, You Can't Have Israel!
Lights in the Darkness
The Seven Feasts of Israel
Netanyahu
Jew-Hatred and the Church
The Visionaries
Why Was I Born?

TO PURCHASE, CONTACT: orders@timeworthybooks.com
P. O. BOX 30000, PHOENIX, AZ 85046